# The Emerging Leader

# The Emerging Leader

*Stepping Up in Leadership*

Peter Shaw and Colin Shaw

CANTERBURY
PRESS
Norwich

© Peter Shaw and Colin Shaw 2013

First published in 2013 by the Canterbury Press Norwich
Editorial office
3rd Floor, Invicta House,
108–114 Golden Lane,
London EC1Y 0TG.

Canterbury Press is an imprint of Hymns Ancient & Modern Ltd
(a registered charity)
13A Hellesdon Park Road, Norwich,
Norfolk, NR6 5DR, UK

www.canterburypress.co.uk

British Library Cataloguing in Publication data

A catalogue record for this book is available
from the British Library

978 1 84825 329 2

Typeset by Manila Typesetting Company
Printed and bound in Great Britain by
CPI Group (UK) Ltd, Croydon

# Contents

*To Holly Shaw, an inspiring spouse and generous daughter-in-law, who is gifted at enabling others to grow as leaders.*

# Acknowledgements

Writing this book has been an excellent father and son bonding exercise. Thankfully we have been in agreement about what we wanted to say. We wanted to acknowledge each other's contribution, with Colin providing lots of ideas and Peter fine-tuning the text. Peter wants to thank his colleagues at Praesta Partners and the range of people he has worked with individually and in groups and teams, who have always kept him fresh and brought new insights and experiences.

Colin wants to thank his former colleagues at Barclays Capital for the faith they put in him allowing him to take on opportunities that developed and stretched him as an emerging leader. He wants to thank his current colleagues for their support and encouragement as a young leader within a fast-moving international consultancy practice.

We both want to acknowledge the contribution of Jackie Tookey, who has typed most of the manuscript with immense patience and fortitude. We are grateful to Helen Burtenshaw, who has helped organize the material into its coherent whole with care and skill.

We are grateful to Christine Smith for commissioning the book and for her encouragement as we wrote it. We appreciate her belief in this book as an innovative project written by a father and a son. We also appreciate the comments of those who have read the draft text and in particular the helpful insights from Marc Gilbert and Alex Hall.

We want to thank Iain McMillan for writing the Foreword of the book. Iain has placed a strong and consistent emphasis on the development of emerging leaders in Scotland, emphasizing the importance of the ambition to make a difference.

We particularly appreciate the support of members of our family. Any wisdom we have normally comes from Frances in her role as spouse and mother. Graham and Ruth are a constant source of stories and practical common sense. We have dedicated the book to Holly, who always brings energy and thoughtfulness. We are grateful to her for her willingness to let her husband and father-in-law disappear off to write the book.

Our final acknowledgement is to all those emerging leaders we know. We want to encourage them to be the best they can be as they take on the full mantle of the responsibility of leadership.

# Foreword

Organizations that thrive are always growing and nurturing future leaders. An organization that stifles new leaders, stunts their growth or attempts to turn them into clones of their archetypal current leaders is destined to die.

Emerging leaders need opportunities to show what they can do, take responsibility and deliver the organization's goals. They need to be encouraged to stretch their understanding, extend their knowledge and develop new skills in new ways. They need the opportunity to experiment and develop their strengths in leading and motivating others.

Emerging leaders need to be given responsibility and experience in testing situations, so that they are prepared and equipped to become the next generation of senior leaders. Asking for responsibility, making known in the right way their ambitions to make a difference, and developing clarity about their own personal development objectives and how to achieve them are the hallmarks of tomorrow's leaders. Emerging leaders recognize that they are responsible for the development of their own careers.

This book is a valuable guide to those who are emerging leaders and those who are enabling emerging leaders to grow into their full potential. For example, as you step up a level, the book provides a clear set of prompts about clarifying your mission and setting direction, positioning yourself as an influencer, taking responsibility for your own actions, making tough decisions and handling conflict well.

What is so distinctive about this book is the way it brings together an experienced leader, coach and business-school professor, with an emerging leader. Peter has had significant leadership roles in the public, private and voluntary sectors, including three posts as a director general. His books have been an inspiration to many leaders. Colin, Peter's son, is an emerging leader with valuable cross-sector experience in international banking, the voluntary sector, international sport (where he has represented Great Britain) and consultancy.

Their book combines the wisdom of experience and the energy of youth. They have created a powerful cocktail of ideas and practical suggestions, with questions at the end of each chapter that enable the reader to reflect on the content of the book as it applies to his or her own unique circumstances. The book is an essential read for those who aspire to be emerging leaders or have had leadership responsibilities thrust upon them.

Reading the book gave me a new perspective, greater knowledge of leadership characteristics and renewed energy to recalibrate my own ambitions for the future. I am sure that reading it will do the same for you.

As you read the book and discuss it with colleagues and friends, allow yourself to be stimulated by the ideas. They will enable you to sharpen the focus on your own next steps as an emerging leader.

Iain M. McMillan CBE
Director, CBI Scotland

# Introduction

You may have been appointed to take on project leadership responsibilities for the first time. You might be a leader of a team in the voluntary, public or private sectors. You may be a newly appointed head of department in a secondary school or a deputy head in a primary school. You might be leading a finance team in a company. You might be a newly appointed curate, minister or incumbent in a church. You might have taken on leadership responsibilities on a voluntary basis within a charity in an inner-city area.

Great! You have worked hard to get to this position. You are excited by the opportunity that this role gives you to make a difference in your chosen sphere. But a few days later you can feel apprehensive and inadequate. What have you taken on? How do you make a difference when you have limited experience? Your confidence oscillates up and down like a yoyo.

This book is for those stepping up in leadership. You are one of the emerging leaders who are essential for the long-term success of any organization. You are bound to experience a cacophony of emotions. One moment you are elated and the next you might be daunted.

Previously you will have been responsible for your own, personal contribution. Now you have greater responsibility for leading other people. You have accountability rather than being someone else's assistant. As you reflect on these responsibilities, they are joyful prospects one minute and a potential burden the next.

You are excited about the challenges that leadership brings, but you are not sure where to focus. You have some nervousness about how you will respond in tough situations. You are looking for a practical guide that will help you think through what you need to do to make a success of your responsibilities. You want to take it a step at a time and want to do well.

Perhaps you are thinking of applying to take on a leadership role. You feel apprehensive and want to apply, but you are not sure whether you have the competence or confidence to do the role well. You are looking for a practical book that will help you build your confidence and readiness for taking on a leadership role for the first time. You want to seek greater responsibility, but doubts and apprehensions are getting in the way.

This book will help you be clear about the strengths you bring. It will give you an understanding of how best to use those skills to inspire and motivate those around you. It will help you nurture those strengths and identify and develop areas for improvement.

This book will enable you to develop a clearer understanding of the way forward. You will be able to break down the many challenges of leadership, and each component will become more readily manageable.

This book will inspire you to engage more fully with those around you and lead them to achieve greater things, building your legacy in the process.

We have divided this book into eight parts. Each can be read separately, so feel free to go to parts that look especially relevant for you. The first four parts relate particularly to the first stages of taking on a leadership role, and look at understanding yourself and those you work with, making early progress, enjoying the journey and knowing your foibles. The second half focuses on establishing yourself as a leader after the initial phase. It looks at moving up a level, keeping alert, embedding your learning and taking next steps.

Reading this book will throw up ideas and spark new trains of thought in your head. It is important to give yourself the space to be stimulated by and engage with these ideas. This book is not a blueprint for your next steps; it is a catalyst for your own learning. Try to apply everything you learn to your own situation. At the end of each chapter we have included a number of reflection questions. Take some time to work through these questions as they relate to your current or future situation. If helpful, talk through the questions with a friend.

If you have been inspired to pick up this book, we believe you have every potential to make a lasting difference as an emerging leader. With time and focus you will go on to achieve great things!

Every great leader was once an emerging leader. The journey starts here.

Peter Shaw
*Godalming*
peter.shaw@praesta.com

Colin Shaw
*East London*
shawcp@gmail.com

# PART I

# Understand yourself and those you work with

As you take on a significant leadership role, your first inclination may be to get stuck in and make a difference, but perhaps the first phase is about standing still and observing, so that you build an understanding of yourself and those you work with. This period of reflection is crucial, so that as you enter a job, you go into it with some awareness of the match between you and the role.

This part looks in turn at knowing your strengths, understanding the context, watching and observing others and preparing your way forward.

# I

# Know your strengths

You may feel ill-equipped for this role and anxious about how you will do it. But others believe in you and have appointed you. They saw strengths in you that you might not fully appreciate.

You may have been appointed because people saw potential in you based on what you have done already. You may have been appointed because you bring complementary skills and understanding to the team.

Your youth or relative inexperience might have been a key reason for your appointment. They want your energy and freshness to infuse the whole team. Your self-perception might be that you do not bring many strengths as a leader, but all of us have been in a position of leadership. Encouraging a friend to think seriously about a particular job opportunity is a form of leadership that enables someone to think through their own next steps. Contacting someone to invite them to go with you to the theatre is a small act of leadership.

If you write down your strengths, and put excessive modesty on one side, you will be surprised about how many strengths you have. If you ask your friends at what are the qualities they most admire in you, you are likely to be embarrassed by the richness of what they say. We can often be far too modest for our own good.

It is worth reflecting on the transferable skills you bring. In the work environment, you might feel young and inexperienced. In a sports team, you might be the person team members look to for a lead. On the sports field you know how to encourage, steer and even direct. Those are skills that can be readily transferable into the work environment.

Being strong does not mean you always need to know the answer. Knowing your strengths is about asking good questions and drawing out the best in others. In the long run, the capability to bring out the best in others is far more valuable than a personal competence in a thousand and one different things.

When you bring a particular contribution as an expert, feel free to make that contribution, because that is the strength you bring. But always have a careful eye to how being an expert is interpreted. It can be expressed in either a disempowering or an empowering way. If you are not an expert, do not pretend to be one as it will not take long for others to realize your pretence. It is far better to ask a good question than to pretend to have expertise that is not there.

It is always worth asking the question: Why have I been appointed as a leader? What were the reasons why this decision was made? Is it because I'm a specialist or a good manager or a good member of the team? It is helpful to reflect on why people will be listening to you, or not. If you are not clear why you have been appointed, ask.

You may be nervous about becoming a leader for a number of different reasons. Perhaps you have not done this type of role before or you have not had experience of this particular context before. Perhaps you are nervous about how people will interpret your leadership contribution. But remember: they may be as nervous as you. You can take the first step in enabling people to feel at home with you by the strength of how you welcome and engage with them in those early stages.

---

*Alex had just been appointed to lead a new project team imple-
menting a computing system in a large firm. He had a strong
track record as an expert, but was new to leadership. He knew
that he had to switch from personal performance to working*

*effectively through others. As he reflected on how he was going to lead his team, he talked with friends he played hockey with. They helped him appreciate his qualities in motivating members of the hockey team. Alex knew he had to draw on his strength both as an expert and as a good motivator of people outside work. He had got good feedback about why he had been appointed to the role and recognized that he need not be shy about the reasons why he had been promoted.*

# For reflection

- What do you see as the key strengths you bring to the role you are in?
- What are the transferable skills you bring from other spheres of your life?
- What would others see as your strengths that you might not fully recognize?

## 2

# Understand the context

When you start a new role, those appointing you will have painted a picture about what needs to be done. You may have had the opportunity to triangulate that view talking to other people, or you may have been restricted from doing so. The context may, at first, seem clear, but there are inevitably many different perspectives rather than one single truth.

You may have been painted a rosy picture because those appointing wanted to attract good quality applicants. You may have seen a more depressing perspective – individuals stuck in their ways and not seeing opportunities ahead.

Understanding the context means getting as many different views as you can about what is the current reality and what might be the next steps. The mix of perspectives of your staff, other colleagues, customers and members of the organization will give a wealth of understanding. Do not expect everyone to have the same view. It would be deeply worrying if they did!

Any new leader needs to understand the history of their particular team or organization. What have been the tragedies or battles that the team has gone through? What are the scars that are still there? What is the folk history about successes or about times of renewal and enjoyment that are still sources of encouragement? Knowing and recognizing the history of the team or organization can help you become accepted as you build on that legacy in a constructive way.

It is important to gain a perspective about whether a group or team you are going to lead is regarded as successful or failing.

Are you building on a good platform, or is upwards the only direction that you can take your team? Is there a burning issue that needs to be addressed straightaway, with an impending crisis if action is not taken? Do you have time to observe and understand the dynamics more before you need to take strong action?

Part of understanding the context is recognizing whether people are looking to you to spoon-feed them. Do they want a directive type of leader, or a leader who will be an enabler and stimulator of others? Most groups will have a mixture of people, some of whom want a directive leader and others an enabling leader. The skill is discerning what the balance is between those two requirements, both in what people say and what their actions demonstrate they really want; it is balancing adaptability to the context and the people, alongside being authentic to your strengths.

Understanding the context includes recognizing what people are looking to you for as their leader. They may be looking for someone who can give them a sense of purpose and help them sort out priorities. They may be looking for a leader who can protect them from the whims of clients or the unreasonable demands of senior people within the organization.

A good question to ask of yourself is: What one or two things can I do that will make the biggest difference to the success of this team? The responses can shed valuable light on the expectations people have and the context in which you will be operating.

Understanding the context is also about recognizing that you may well have under your authority people who are older and more experienced than you. Success comes through recognizing their experience and drawing upon it, while being rooted in your understanding about why you have been appointed. It is important not to try to pretend that you are more experienced than other people, while at the same time explicitly drawing on your own experience and insights so that together you find a constructive way forward.

> Alex had a few team members with strong views who were quick to make their opinions heard. He made sure he sought the perspectives of everyone on the team, to understand the full context. It took time and energy to draw out the opinions of the quieter members, but their perspective proved invaluable in setting his approach. Once he understood where everyone was coming from, he could develop a clear way forward. Although his solutions didn't always please everyone, each team member appreciated their part in the process and felt their views were being heard.

## For reflection

- What elements of the history of your team or group do you need to build on?
- What aspects of the wider context need gripping and sorting first?
- How do you balance the range of perspectives you have received, some of which are optimistic while others are discouraging about future prospects?

# 3

# Watch and observe others

Watching and observing others is about drawing on the experience of those who have been successful and those less successful. If you want to be a head teacher you are likely to have a wealth of experience about what makes a good head teacher and what results in their being less successful. Before you take on a new role, it can be helpful to reflect on people who have held similar roles in the past and what have been the generic characteristics of those who have been successful. Who caught your imagination and inspired you when they were leaders? What attributes did you most admire?

Conversely, reflecting on someone who was in leadership over you when you had a negative experience can be a powerful source of learning about what motivates. Walking through your emotions as you reflect on a leader who had a negative impact on you can reinforce your understanding of the pitfalls you want to avoid. It can be equally helpful to observe those leaders in similar roles now to the one you are moving into. What do they do that works well? How have they built up the competence and confidence of their team? When is that positive difference just about good fortune or can you learn from their approach and adopt good practice from it?

Observing members of the team can give you insights into when people's energy is at its highest or at its lowest. How do people recharge themselves? How consistent is their approach and behaviour? What throws them off track and creates a spiral downwards?

Asking yourself when members of your organization appear to work well together and when less well together can give you insights into the dynamics. Knowing the history of the interrelationships can give you a perspective on when there are encouragements that can be built on further, and how best you can intervene.

Every organization has its own internal politics. It is important to understand these internal dynamics without being obsessed or ruled by them. Building an insight into the internal politics helps develop a sensitivity about which battles to avoid and which alliances to be mindful of. Having a careful eye on who is seeking influence helps you decide who to build partnerships with.

Parallels can always be drawn from other areas of life that give insights into a team or group that you lead. Watching the dynamic in a sports team, community group or family can give a continuous flow of examples of when individuals and teams work well together and when they destabilize each other.

It is not just about watching and observing others. It is about watching and observing yourself. What is the impact you have on others? When does a suggestion from you drop like a heavy stone straight to the bottom, or when does a suggestion from you create a ripple that influences the thinking of everyone in the team? Notice when you enthuse or when you depress others in all areas of life, be it at home, in the community or at work.

Everyone else will be watching and observing you as the leader. They will note your energy levels and demeanour. Their natural inclination will be to mirror how you act and behave. If you are positive and encouraging, they are likely to be the same. If you are downhearted, they will become even more downhearted than you. Others will be observing how you respond to difficulties and disagreements. If you brush these under the carpet, they will want to do the same. If you are honest and open in handling difficult situations and recognizing different views, they will have the courage to do the same.

> *Alex took time to observe and understand how they responded to him as the leader. He needed to give them space to be themselves and not be overawed by his presence or be trying to impress him. In a parallel project within the firm, the leader had generated a highly motivated and successful team. Alex sought to understand what the keys of that team's success were, and tried to embody the characteristics that would suit his situation. He reflected on the successes and limitations of other leaders he had worked under. The process helped improve his confidence in developing a clear way forward. Alex was conscious that he was being watched, so he kept a consistent, positive and thoughtful demeanour that was open about the difficulties but always positive about the opportunities.*

## For reflection

- What are you particularly watching and observing in the team and the wider organization?
- What is your learning from watching those in similar leadership positions?
- What will others be watching and observing in you?

# 4

# Prepare your way forward

Preparing your way forward is about bringing the best of your previous experience alongside understanding the context you are now operating within and the views and expectations of others. Preparing your way forward is rarely about providing a precise blueprint that you prepared earlier. Imposing a model that may have worked well in one context straight into another is likely to be a recipe for aggravation and discord.

Sometimes there will be fixed points about which you have clear views. But without good evidence to underpin those views and the support of some key others, you are unlikely to build agreement about the way forward.

Leaders who create momentum are often those who demonstrate they are building on past success, even though they might be encouraging a sharp change of direction. You may have an ideal way forward, but a key question might be: If I draw out the preferences of others, will they be near enough to the direction I would like to travel in? You may have an ideal way forward. You can be comfortable with a range of possibilities that come from others that are within the broad parameters of what you think is the best way forward.

Preparing your way forward is about creating a set of expectations in others about what is possible and on what timescale. Sometimes dropping in or sounding out suggestions with a range of different people can help create a climate of opinion about what is doable. If some trusted members of the team say to you that certain outcomes are attainable, sharing that perspective across the whole team can create a raised set of expectations across the whole team.

Preparing the way can include building an assumption that some decisions do need to be taken on a tight timescale. This is not about bouncing people into submission, it is sharing evidence about the necessity for some early decisions, particularly where it is increasingly clear that issues about finance, priorities or personnel need to be resolved within a short timescale. Sometimes action is going to be needed whether people like it or not. As a leader, it is necessary to ensure these actions happen while carrying people with you as best you can. Key to this is effective communication about why steps are needed, particularly if they are counter to people's preferences.

Building a shared vision about the longer term is also a necessary part of preparing a way forward. A vision that gives a sense of purpose that is both ambitious and realistic is central to providing a cohesive sense of direction. Sometimes it is not possible to define a clear vision for the future because of a wide range of uncertainties. But a combination of being precise where possible and being honest about what is uncertain, can encourage a good balance between ambition and practical realism. Sometimes the overall vision will be determined from above, and your role will be to share that vision in an engaging way and to develop your own perspective as a team about how you fit in with this bigger picture.

A few weeks after starting a new role can be an ideal time to reflect on where you are headed. What are the good things you want to build on and what do you need to change? You have to judge what changes are needed and how much of that can evolve anyway, how much is by stealth, how much is by creating a different set of expectations in others and how much has to be tackled head on. For your own sanity, the period of reflection needs to lead to an affirmation about what is going well and what you are building on, as well as a clarity about difficult judgements you need to make and how you are going to take them forward.

> *Alex rapidly came to the view that the team needed to change its priorities. He was hearing a similar view from a number of members of the team and was therefore able to base his proposal to change the priorities on what he had heard from other people. It was not Alex imposing from outside. He was very deliberately rebalancing priorities and ensuring there was greater focus on the areas he judged were particularly important. After he had been in post for a month, Alex took time out to reflect for half a day. It was clear to him that he needed to make some short-term decisions, including moving on a member of the team. But he also needed to build a shared view about the outcomes the project team leader needed to deliver by the end of the year. He set up a half-day event to build agreed expectations about outcomes within a year.*

## For reflection

- How best do you build on what is going well in the organization?
- How do you create a set of expectations for the future that are ambitious and to which people are committed?
- What issues need sorting quickly and what tough decisions need to be made?

# PART 2

# Making progress

This part explores some of the early stages in establishing yourself in a significant leadership role over the first twelve months. The initial excitement is there alongside being a touch daunted by the issues you face. You are conscious that these first steps are quite important as you take on the mantle of leadership. Like a new coat, it fits but does not yet feel entirely comfortable. You know it is going to be one step at a time. You are conscious that you should not rush these first steps, but know that you need to make progress and begin to establish yourself as the leader.

This part looks in turn at growing your supporters, building your team, living with your wobbles and giving thanks for signs of progress.

# 5

# Grow your supporters

You may feel alone and exposed as a new leader. But someone appointed you. They believed in you or they would not have put you into this leadership role.

You may be surprised how many supporters you have. They will not be clapping your appearance every time you walk down the same corridor, but there will be a quiet respect and admiration that may not be visible but is there to be built on.

Some will be identifying with you and want you to do well. Some may have known you for some time, and you have built up a strong relationship. Others have observed you from a distance and like you and respect you. Perhaps you said a word of encouragement to them that you now do not remember, but they have not forgotten your kindness. Some people may be your supporters for extraneous reasons, such as your support of the same football team or sharing similar social interests.

It is always worth considering who is likely to be committed to your success. This is likely to include those who appointed you, those who will benefit from your doing well and those who regard you in some way or another as an ally or as a role model. Even the grumpiest of people can be your supporters. They may not be effusive in their manner but they will be watching you and ready to support you when they begin to see an attitude or approach that is going to make a constructive difference.

When you take on a new role, some people will be observing you neutrally and waiting to see what you do and how you do it. How best do you win them over? What matters in the early stages of a relationship is about listening, observing and summarizing what you have seen and heard.

A key way of winning supporters is through your tone and approach. If your tone is engaging, warm and encouraging, while asking thoughtful questions, this will begin to generate a sense of engagement, and those you are talking with will want to support you. Building support comes from taking action where it is needed. The new leader who is seen to want to grip a difficult problem will be admired, provided they do not rush to an impetuous answer. Most organizations welcome a new leader who listens well and is selective in handling urgent issues that have festered.

Building your supporters in the early stages will mean differentiating how you build key relationships. With some, the support will result from focused conversations, with others it will be shared stories, while with others it will be open-ended discussion about future possibilities. The way you build support will include recognition of the experience and personalities of those you are working with.

After a while it will be clear who will speak up on your behalf. They are to be encouraged and nurtured, but you will want to resist the temptation to form cliques in a public way. The wider your support the better, but at the same time, build partnerships and alliances with individuals whom you trust. When you sense that someone is not your supporter, it is worth trying to win them over. Perhaps this is best done via an informal coffee, going for a walk together at lunchtime or trying to find a project you can work on together.

Sometimes a critic has to be ignored. But if you sense scepticism in someone, the earlier that is discussed and talked through the better. Understanding the reasons for their criticism may give you valuable insights. Inevitably, there will be two or three people whom you do not regard as your supporters and have not so far been able to convert. Try to keep up a warm and open approach while ensuring that your wellbeing does not depend on the approval of these individuals. Keep trying to understand where they are coming from but do not allow yourself to be emotionally dependent on a successful outcome. It will be important to establish a working relationship with them, whether it is built on shared understanding or respect.

> *Sunita had just been appointed to lead an audit team working with a series of departments in a large private organization. Some of the directors were delighted to see an energetic and thoughtful younger person appointed to this job. Others were less sure as Sunita had limited experience. They did not want this bright young thing trying to exert herself by demonstrating they were wrong and she was right. The directors feared she might be too diffident or overly dogmatic. Most of the directors were pleasantly surprised. Sunita wanted to talk and listen to them. She asked good questions and didn't seem to prejudge them. One or two continued to be sceptical and reserve their positions, but most had been won over by Sunita's attitude in the first month.*

# For reflection

- Who are the supporters you need to thank and nurture?
- Who might become your supporters if you cultivate them carefully?
- Who might not be your supporters and how are you going to handle them?

# 6

# Build your team

You will be inheriting team dynamics and politics, some which will be healthy and some unhealthy. The people you inherit will inevitably be a mixture. You will have had good reports of some and more hesitant comments about others. You will want to make your own judgements and not be prejudiced by the perspectives of other people.

Your predecessor might have given you valuable insights, but truth has many angles and you might be able to bring the best out in someone who was not highly thought of by your predecessor. As you talk with the members of your team, keep an eye on their responsiveness and adaptability. How set in their ways are they? How are they going to respond to your priorities and the tone you are setting?

You will build an early sense of how the team is working together. Sometimes your open questions can help unblock issues and enable a new way forward to be identified. It is important to be sensitive that some people may have been looking forward to your appointment and will have expectations about changes you will introduce. Your arrival might mean that some members of the team want to reopen issues, resulting in a set of conversations that energize some and depress others.

You will want to observe how well people listen to each other. How complementary are people in bringing different skills to the team and is there a sense of mutual engagement and listening?

An individual can be an excellent rugby player but not fit well into a team. For a team to play well, the individuals have to know their own strengths and also appreciate and play to the strengths of others. A rugby player who is too much of an individualist and does not build partnership effectively with other players is likely to have a de-motivating effect on the whole team, hence the importance of observing within your team who motivates other members of the team successfully and who saps their energy. Some team members may have relatively low self-esteem and need to develop their individual contributions.

A good rowing eight has to act in time. The rhythm is obvious and needs to be adhered to. A good negotiating team will include people playing different roles, but they have to understand what the other contributors are doing and how best they ensure a successful outcome. You may well want to begin to set some expectations about how you want the team to work together. You will want to reinforce the good things that each team member brings. You will want to build up the quality of the relationship between you and them as individuals so there is a shared agenda and a joint understanding of what are successful outcomes.

You may want to have an early conversation with the team about shared outcomes and approaches. You will want to begin to build a perspective about what will bring out the best of each member of the team and what is the value-added contribution each person can bring that will help the team as a whole to be successful.

It can be helpful to see yourself having a distinct relationship with individual team members and with the team as a whole. With the individual team members, you will be varying your style and nature of challenge depending on their personality and the challenges in their area, but with the team as a whole there needs to be a consistent approach even though each member of the team will be looking for something different from you.

Building your team is about creating clarity about what they are going to achieve and how it is going to be done. It is creating a stretch that comes from an agreed way forward rather than an imposed requirement. Success comes from participants being willing to take responsibility for what the team does. Successful teams enjoy each other's company, recognize the complementary skills of different participants, acknowledge each other's contribution and stretch each other so that the outcome is 'more than the sum of the parts'.

Building your team might well include having hard conversations with those people who do not look as if they are pulling their weight. Setting clear expectations will be part of building your team. Creating a situation where people can move on with honour may well be necessary.

You will need to build the best possible team to achieve the goals you have been set. This is likely to be mainly through building the commitment of those people you inherit. When there is an opportunity to recruit, it is worth devoting as much time as is needed to get the right new members of the team. If you are doubtful about potential new recruits, the answer is probably that it is best not to recruit them.

---

*Sunita inherited a mixed group of auditors. Some of her team were set in their ways while others were keen to experiment with new approaches. She had a session with the team, looking at their priorities over the next few months. It was a desultory conversation with little interaction or creativity. Sunita knew she had to try a different tack. She asked all members of the team to talk about what they needed from other members in order to bring out the best in themselves. This sparked off a good discussion. Sunita latched on to some of the points that were being made and she sensed there was now a breakthrough. There could be a common purpose in building the team's reputation in different parts of the organization and improving their professional competence and reputation. Sunita began to conclude that one or two people needed to move on, but she could work with the rest of them.*

# For reflection

- What would bring out the best in each member of your team?
- What is hindering team development and how can that be overcome?
- What are the complementary skills in the team that could be further developed?

# 7

# Live with your wobbles

Your confidence will be high one minute and take a dip the next. You think that you understand the issues clearly, and then someone makes a comment that shows that your understanding is only partial.

It feels like you are putting the jigsaw together slowly. Certain areas are taking shape, with huge areas of blankness in other parts of the jigsaw, but gradually, as each piece is fitted into the whole, the overall picture becomes clearer. It has to be one step at a time, but then there are flashes of insight as you begin to grasp some of the key implications and sense what might be the best way forward.

You will experience wobbles. That is a fact of life. If you do not experience wobbles it is likely you are being insensitive to some of the difficult issues and perspectives. But when you have a wobble it is worth treating it as valuable data. What is the wobble telling you about issues or people that need to be handled with care?

When your confidence begins to drop, stop and reflect on similar situations in the past that you have been able to handle well. How did you deal with those wobbles? The approaches that have worked for you in the past are likely to be helpful going forward.

Experience from being part of a family or sports team can help. In every family there will be unsettling incidents. No sports team is going to win every match. There are always going to be reverses when the team that has been defeated needs to take stock. It may mean they decide to change their approach or they might conclude their approach was right, but they were having a bad day or the opposition was particularly good. If every reverse is seen as a valuable learning experience, then the experience, although initially seen as a defeat, can be a means of strengthening the way an individual or team will handle similar situations in the future.

It can be helpful to see a wobble in a longer-term context. You might not remember the wobble in twelve months, as its significance may be much less than it currently appears.

As you begin to plan for the future, it is worth recognizing that the best laid plans can go wrong. The ideal balance is to have a clear resolve to make the progress you want, while at the same time recognizing that living with reverses is part of life. You win some and lose some. What matters is winning enough.

Part of living with your wobbles is recognizing that a leadership role comes with responsibilities. You are accountable for the actions you take, and sometimes things go wrong. What matters is preparing for the risks as well as possible while not allowing the thought of risks to stifle creativity and inhibit necessary action.

If your approach is that you are going to be the best leader you can be, you are less likely to be hit by debilitating crises of confidence. If we strive for perfection, we are likely to be disappointed. If our aim is to do the best job we can, we are more likely to pass a threshold where we are both pleased and comfortable with the outcome.

It can be helpful to hold in your mind examples of people who have suffered reverses and how they have come through successfully: for example, recovering from a family disagreement or dispute within a sports team. Often they have been able to talk about what went wrong in a calm and measured way and point clearly to their learning. Being as straightforward and rational as possible reassures you and those around you that emotionally you can handle things going wrong.

If you do not expect the world of other people, they will not expect the world of you. If you do not expect people to be perfect, they will not expect you to be perfect. If you talk about your mistakes and what you have learnt from them, that can reassure your people that you are human too. If you can enable your team to live with and learn from their wobbles, you are enabling them to mature and deal with subsequent issues well.

Sometimes if you are wobbling with uncertainty about what to do next, it is a matter of following your intuitive sense about building consensus or being directive about the way forward. If you can sit alongside your wobble with the confidence that 'I can do it', then you can move beyond the wobble. That determination will then cascade down through others, whose natural reaction will be to mirror your behaviour. If you demonstrate a positive belief that you can take on the leadership challenges successfully, then those around you are likely to adopt a similar self-belief.

---

*Sunita felt she was making good progress, but after a few weeks her confidence began to sag. She did not feel that she had a sure touch. Some of her judgements seemed to be being criticized. Her hesitancy grew in some situations, but she remembered how she had coped with wobbles in previous roles. She knew she had to hold her nerve, believe she could do the job well, continue to listen to others and be willing to talk constructively about how she intended to approach the challenges ahead. Sunita knew she had to stand up tall, be alert to the risks and then follow her intuitive sense about next steps. Her confidence enabled the confidence of those she worked with to grow so that the audit issues they were working on could be solved.*

# For reflection

- What type of wobbles are you most likely to have and where might they come from?
- From previous experience, how best do you handle those wobbles?
- How best do you prepare for the next dip in confidence when it comes your way?

# 8

# Give thanks for signs of progress

Give thanks joyfully for the progress you are making. Allow yourself to celebrate in whatever way works for you. Acknowledge small steps and don't just wait for the big leaps.

The bricklayer can readily admire their work as the wall is constructed. There are immediate signs of progress that can be acknowledged. After the gardener has planted rows of seeds, there is nothing visible to celebrate with the seeds hidden well below ground. But all of a sudden there is progress as green shoots burst through and then a few months later there are crops to harvest.

Sometimes it is right to celebrate alone. The boss agreed to your recommendation or the client was grateful for the piece of work you had initiated. Marking that progress must be right to do as you build your reputation and confidence in a new role, one brick at a time, even if it is only in giving yourself a five-minute break or a metaphorical pat on the back.

Giving thanks for signs of progress is both about what you say to yourself and what you say to other people. Your staff and colleagues will be watching how you respond to them. Do you thank them, and when you thank them is it for specific reasons? The utterance of general words of thanks can wear thin after a while, but when they are related to specific contributions they are much more likely to carry conviction and be regarded as significant.

It is always right to recognize people's contributions through thanks. This is all the more important when rewarding them with bonuses or when promotion is not an option.

Thanks can be private recognition or public acknowledgement, which reinforces the sense of direction and energy within a team. The public acknowledgement might involve buying doughnuts for the team or a celebratory bottle of wine. The costs of an 'unproductive' hour spent celebrating are likely to be outweighed by the long-term benefits.

As you thank your staff for specific contributions you are reinforcing their belief that that is the right type of contribution to make. By virtue of not explicitly thanking them for other contributions you are reducing the significance of those contributions.

Giving thanks is not just about indulgence and gratification over a long period. It is about taking key steps and moving forward confidently believing that the next challenges can be overcome too.

Tiny bits of progress can be so valuable. When you begin to change attitudes it can be the start of a new momentum. As signs of progress become stronger, there will be better indications of what is likely to work or not work in the future. These indications give you valuable insights about where you want to push next. Where there is progress, there are going to be other doors to open. When someone begins to open up to you and wants to build a common cause, there is the opportunity for shared projects or activities that will lead to a win/win.

In a new post you may want to revolutionize the outcomes or reputation of a particular team. The level of the competence of the team needs to go up a few steps, but it is one step at a time. The reputation of the team needs to become stronger. You need a few people to speak out in support of what you and your people are doing. Once your reputation begins to creep up and the curve has changed direction, that is the moment to give thanks, even if there are just first indications of progress and there is a long way still to go.

> *Sunita was thrilled with progress after the first few weeks. Her boss had even said thank you for some particular pieces of work. The attitude of some of her clients had begun to change from being cynical to showing a more constructive approach. Her team was showing a bit more enthusiasm than before. Sunita made a point of taking time to thank her team when they had made progress. She knew that people listened to what she said and the tone of her voice. This was a powerful tool that she knew she could use to build the strength of shared endeavour. Sunita reminded herself to thank those people who had helped her build up her confidence to take on this new role. Their faith in her had been crucial as she embarked on this next step in her leadership journey.*

## For reflection

- Are you giving thanks enough for signs of progress?
- Are you thanking people enough and in a way that acknowledges the right attitudes and behaviours?
- Who might you thank who has helped build your confidence?

PART 3

# Enjoying the journey

This part explores enjoying the journey. The responsibilities can feel daunting. The risks of things going wrong can feel acute. You may be overwhelmed by uncertainty and your confidence may dip. What can help is being able to smile at the journey you are on, and allowing yourself to be excited about the possibilities. Building a shared expectation with others can generate hope and energy. Being alert to what gives you energy or saps your energy is so important in helping you get your rhythms right. Part of the journey will be stepping into the unknown: the more you can enjoy that sense of adventure the better. Our hope is that this part will help raise your spirits and enable you to see your world as half full rather than half empty.

# 9

# Allow yourself to be excited

When you applied for this leadership role you were excited about the possibilities. When you were told you had been successful you probably had mixed emotions of being thrilled and daunted at the same time. As you began to get into the role, some of the possibilities seemed less doable or much harder work. It did not feel as straightforward as you had imagined. Sometimes you felt as if you were looking towards sunny uplands; on other occasions it felt like peering through a glass darkly or seeing large, dark clouds ahead.

What can help is to write down what excited you when you were appointed. What did you see then as the possibilities? What was it that you felt you could be passionate about in this role? Some of these opportunities may fade while others may be as important as ever, but can be overlaid by the pressures of the day or uncertainties about the future.

Allowing yourself to be too excited about what might be possible in a particular role can be self-delusion. But unless we are excited and passionate, progress will be slow and unrewarding. Keeping asking questions about what the possibilities are, what you are passionate about and what is beginning to excite you is so important in order to keep up your resolve.

What might excite you can come from observing what is happening in other, similar organizations and seeing what can be transferred into your team. Asking others in similar situations what are their causes of excitement and what are the possibilities for them can stimulate a freshness of thinking. Seeing an issue with fresh eyes can mean that you see linkages and opportunities for partnership to which others have become immune.

Moving into a different physical environment either as an individual or a team can help create new stimulus. If you always sit around a table, try sitting in a circle with no table as a barrier between you. If you always have discussions sitting down, try standing up and moving around. If your key discussions are always in the same room, try moving into a different physical space, which may not be in the same building. If you always meet in the afternoon, try meeting in the morning. Building in variety can create a freshness that can mean possibilities become more real and more exciting.

Picturing in your mind what the organization or team might look like in a year or two can help build the excitement and motivation about the steps necessary to reach that outcome. Asking a team to describe the words they would hope others would use to describe them can reinforce a desire to move in that direction. If the team wants to be described as responsive by its customers, that aspiration can create a desire to move purposefully to become more responsive.

If you can picture the excitement of a successful outcome, this can feed back into the desire to set milestones along the way and reach those milestones.

So often when resources are tight there is a natural inclination to look inwards and see barriers rather than opportunities. But asking hard questions when resources are tight can often mean that changes that had been thought impossible are reconsidered. Certain routines or restrictive practices are now open to question. The tightness of resources can paradoxically lead to a greater willingness to take up opportunities and do things differently. But unless you have a picture about what doing things differently might mean, it is easy to founder in a stormy sea rather than see the encircling waves and wind as an opportunity to chart a new direction.

Inviting people to think about what the future might look like opens up opportunities. It can be fun, too, to encourage people to dream dreams and envisage what might be delivered by a re-energized team. The more this can be done through creating a sense of adventure and fun, the more likely there will be willing followers rather than reluctant people trailing behind.

---

*Alan had recently been appointed as a vicar. When he was interviewed for the job, he saw a range of possibilities for work with families, the homeless and the wider community, and was excited by the prospect. He could see from his previous experience practical steps that would make a lot of difference. He saw opportunities, but was daunted too. Alan set up an away day, when members of the Parochial Church Council shared their hopes and aspirations and built agreed clarity about key elements that were important to them going forward. There was a renewed vision, which created a sense of excitement and new energy.*

*Alan knew it was an adventure that needed a sense of fun and shared endeavour to ensure there was enough commitment for the possibilities to be realized.*

---

## For reflection

- What particularly excited you when you took on your current role?
- How could you take a step back and see the bigger picture?
- How best do you nurture in yourself the sense of excitement?

# Build shared expectations with others

You believe that particular changes are important or you are clear that a particular blockage needs to be removed. The aim seems abundantly clear. You can get frustrated that others do not see the future as clearly as you do. It is so obvious, you think to yourself, but telling others what to believe is rarely successful. The line 'others ought to think that these changes are right' is more likely to produce apathy than energy.

How best do you create shared expectations with others? It is about listening and demonstrating that you have heard. It is about playing back what you hear of the hopes and aspirations of those people you are working with. Your customers will not buy a particular product because you think it is what they need: they buy the product because they think it is what they need. Therefore, working with the grain of the expectations of customers and clients is crucial to success. Their expectations can be influenced by the freshness of your thinking and the examples you demonstrate, but it is their expectations that matter and not yours.

Building shared expectations with your colleagues is often about you and them looking together at an issue or problem and considering what might be ways forward. The starting point is understanding what matters most to your peers and colleagues, what are the outcomes that are the most important to them, and how you can contribute to enabling them to reach those outcomes.

There will be occasions when preferred expectations will need to be set aside because of prevailing circumstances or an external imperative. The ideal is then to create a set of shared expectations recognizing the limitations about what is possible.

If you are leading a marketing department, how best do you clarify the expectations of your external customers and your internal clients? How best do you work jointly so there is an agreed set of desired outcomes, pathways and products? It may be about sitting down together with a blank sheet of paper and starting with the excitement and expectation of others rather than your own. To the extent that you and others have the same expectations, there is no harm in starting with theirs. There is no particular merit in being the first person to think of an idea if acknowledging the merit of someone else's idea is going to lead to the best outcome.

Those to whom you are accountable will come with their own set of expectations. Sitting down regularly with your boss to ensure that you are seeing shared outcomes is vital for success. When work and life are very busy it is easy for perspectives to move apart. So often we think that we have communicated changed expectations to others, but they have not heard. The boss may have a very different set of pressures upon them and will be looking in another direction most of the time. Hence remembering to check back that you are all on the same page about progress is an essential 'hygiene factor'.

When financial considerations are moving quickly, expectations might well need to change. The risk is that expectations change in your head rather than in dialogue with others. Keeping conversation going about what are the fixed points in expectations and what needs to adapt in the light of changed circumstances is necessary to ensure misunderstandings do not develop.

Whenever a new project is begun, spending time building a set of shared expectations is always worth the investment. All of us come with a particular mindset based on our values and previous experience. Some of these expectations are unsaid and can cause difficulty if they are not brought to the surface. The expectations might be about the type of commitment and involvement you and others are willing to make, as well as about outcomes.

With your own team, it is always worth spending time reflecting on expectations your customers have of you, expectations you have of each other, expectations about outcomes, and your expectations about your individual contributions. Being honest about these expectations, and where they might be in conflict, helps ensure that potential problems are worked through in advance, and can contribute to creating a safe passage.

Building shared expectations is not always about doing what other people want. It can be about shaping what others are suggesting. It might involve setting out some key fixed points, which always has to be done with care. Once you have built up credibility, you can define fixed points and people will go along with you, provided these points are carefully explained, take account of the context and pass a reasonableness test.

---

*Alan was keen for the church to employ a full-time youth worker. He could see clearly the type of contribution one could make, but a key consideration was the expectations of others in the church. Alan was able to contribute some examples of what was working in other places as a stimulus to good discussion. A number of people began to be quite enthusiastic about the idea of having a youth worker, and Alan was able to respond jointly with them in the design of the scheme. He had fed in ideas and key points. He had talked about the value of developing the work with young people; he let the idea evolve so there was a shared understanding about the benefits. He delegated the lead on next steps to a member of the team who was particularly enthusiastic about this idea.*

# For reflection

- How have you been able to build shared expectations with others in the past?
- What is particularly important to you going forward that you could encourage others to develop as an idea?
- What will work best for you in building shared expectations about the future next steps with your colleagues?

# 11

# Be alert to what gives you energy

Our energy is a fluctuating quantity. Sometimes the adrenalin flows and our energy level grows higher and higher. On other occasions our energy is sapped and we seem listless, with no desire or energy to get on with things and make a difference.

Being mindful about what gives you energy can help in designing a working day or week to use that energy to best effect. Asking yourself what gives you energy immediately after lunch can be a practical way of deciding how to use low time to best effect.

Not everything you do will give you energy. There will be boring, routine tasks that need to be done. There will be difficult conversations that need to be taken forward. There will be hard negotiations that will feel joyless and tiring.

Designing your day to spend time with people who give you energy can have spin-off benefits to enable you to tackle the more mundane tasks that drain your energy. It can be helpful to break a day into chunks and calibrate which chunks will give energy and which use the energy that has been generated. Keeping the activities that give and use energy in balance is crucial for our mental and emotional wellbeing.

As you tackle an activity that is using energy, the prospects of what you might be doing later that day or week can be a means of keeping up the momentum. The thought of the walk home, playing with the kids, watching a favourite TV programme or listening to a piece of music can give us the prospect of energy later in the day that can help us keep up energy levels during the demands of a busy day.

The read-across between what gives energy outside work and inside work is important. If you are able to do activities outside work that give you energy, some of that energy will flow into the work situation. So if running gives you energy, do more of it. If spending time with young people lifts your spirits and gives you energy, can you do more of it? If reading a particular type of book energizes you, can you do more of it? In our personal life we are generating energy that can be used across all our different activities. When our batteries run flat, that is the moment to step away and seek to regenerate the energy within you.

What matters is not only what gives you energy but what gives other people energy too. Maybe some of the people you work with get energy from the type of activities that sap your energy. Recognizing the complementarity of others and working with the grain of that difference can bring the satisfaction of working with each other's preferences.

The first question in your mind when thinking about working with your own staff might be about the skills and experience they bring. A key second question might be about how you can enable the energy in people to grow and be expressed in ways that benefit both the organization and them. How to release energy in others and channel that energy in a constructive way is perhaps one of the key leadership questions for any emerging leader.

It is then about channelling energy so it is sensitively steered but not dampened. You probably do not want people's energetic thoughts and ideas coming out in chaotic ways that generate conflict. It is about creating an environment where energy can be released and harnessed, so that it leads to creativity and not friction, and generates new drive rather than well-worn conflict.

Always be observant about the energy levels of people around you. Seek to understand what might be affecting those levels. Is there anything you can do to remove a blockage and release some of that creative energy that is ready and waiting to be used? Well-organized training events or strategy days can help re-energize a team and give it a new sense of direction.

> *Alan was conscious that as a vicar he could easily work twelve hours a day and seven days a week. He knew that what gave him energy was physical activity such as running and hiking. He ensured that in each day he had a burst of physical activity. He led a group from the church on a hiking weekend. Alan knew that good quality conversation with people in the church generated energy in him and them. He created contexts for groups of people to meet together to discuss a range of things from athletics to education to contemporary issues. These conversations gave him energy and helped him and others to work through the relevance of different aspects of their human experience and beliefs. Alan was always mindful about what gave him and others in his community energy. It provided a touchstone for how he approached individual conversations.*

## For reflection

- What work activities give you most energy?
- What rhythms do you want to put in place to use your energy to best effect in order to tackle difficult issues?
- How might you build up the energy levels of those you work with so that together you are stronger than you are as individuals?

## 12

# Enjoy stepping into the unknown

There is a distinctive pleasure in doing a walk you have done before or climbing a mountain that you have tackled success-fully on a previous occasion. But stepping into the unknown brings another set of emotions. Climbing a new mountain brings uncertainties and some risks, but using skills that have worked well before can enable the climb to be tackled with confidence and purpose.

If the work we do means always going through the same type of routine it will soon become dull. Stepping into the unknown provides a sense of excitement, expectation and energy. We never know how good we are at a particular activity until we test it out. If you have never spoken to an audience of 100 people before, you will not know whether you are good at it or not until you take the risk of speaking to a large group. Learn-ing from the experience of speaking to 10 to 20 people can develop both skills and confidence.

When we do our first interview for the local newspaper or local radio, it can feel scary and uncertain. But we can soon develop ways of handling the uncertainty and devise a rhythm to make points clearly in an interview. We have been learning fast from the day we were born.

It is very difficult to stand still. We either keep stepping into the unknown and learning new approaches and new things about ourselves, or we go backwards and lose confidence in our strengths and lose the appetite to try new things. If we stand still for long enough we stiffen up and cannot move forward with any agility. Stepping into the unknown might be about building new partnerships, trying new approaches, overturning previous assumptions, adopting techniques advocated by others.

If we always prepare thoroughly for meetings, it may be a step into the unknown to prepare in more focused ways, identifying the three key points we want to make rather than trying to understand all the details. If when we address an audience we always have a full text, it is a step into the unknown to use abbreviated notes or headlines. As we step into the unknown we can discover new things about ourselves that we might not have appreciated: for example, how well we can speak on an impromptu basis.

Stepping into the unknown is often about testing assumptions. Why have we always done it this way? There might be a very good answer to this, but on other occasions custom and practice have dictated current behaviours that need to change.

We all need time within our comfort zones. But sometimes stretching the boundaries is about being more assertive than is normally our approach. Or it might mean making more effort to build a consensus than would usually be our practice.

As we continue to develop the way we approach issues and widen our repertoire, we are developing in ourselves our set of options. We become less tied to one particular way of doing things. We can then celebrate that we can be either directive or responsive, we can use the innocent question or the direct statement. We can take the lead ourselves or reinforce the contributions of others so that they have the biggest impact.

What can equip you to step out into the unknown is the confidence that you can handle bumps, the backing of those around of you and the adaptability to learn from new challenges.

The people we are working with may be happy for us to step out into the unknown provided they do not have to come too. Sometimes it is right that we go on the 'scout trek' first to find a route, but one of the characteristics of the good leader is that people are willing to follow the leader stepping out into the unknown based on their confidence in the leader's competence and intent.

Taking people with you is so important. You want to be out at the front but not so way out in front that you are separated from your people. Taking people with you is normally a gradual process, although there are points when it all comes together and sceptics become committed followers. When that happens, celebrate how you stepped out into the unknown and then draw people with you.

---

*Alan worked with his Parochial Church Council to develop plans for the future. He was willing to take some risks and step out into the unknown in terms of trying new approaches to the way that the teaching series were put together. He gradually built support through lots of conversations. The leadership team then agreed a new approach that was more coherent and practical. Early feedback was encouraging. Both Alan and the leadership team felt encouraged that they had been willing to step out into the unknown. It was early days but Alan felt he was establishing a pattern of people being willing to think through new ideas and reach a point where they were willing to commit themselves to bring those ideas to fruition.*

---

## For reflection

- When you step out into the unknown, what emotions do you experience and how do you handle them?
- In what ways do you want to set out into the unknown?
- How best are you going to bring people with you as you step out more into the unknown?

# PART 4

# Knowing your foibles

Knowing ourselves and how we react in different circumstances is important as we step up into different leadership roles. We need to be honest with ourselves. Pretending we are fine when we are not can work for a short period. We need to come to terms with issues that are causing us angst and address them.

This part looks at being conscious of your fears, learning how to forgive yourself, being alert to your dreams and being mindful of your foibles and preferences. Living with our foibles is often what we have to do. We are who we are. We can adapt some of our reactions, but we have to live with our personal characteristics, which are often engrained.

Knowing your folk-art

# 13

# Be conscious of your fears

We are all fearful of something. Taking on new responsibilities can bring excitement and energy, but can also lead to anxiety, stress and a touch of fear. These are not necessarily negative experiences, but they have the power to overwhelm. Understanding and managing our fears reduces the chance of panic and enables us to manage risk.

Fear can have positive consequences. Without the fear of being hit by a car, we may not look before crossing the road. A touch of fear can lead us to plan and calculate risks before taking action. But fear also has the power to trap us and cause us to lose clarity. To focus too closely on fears can be overwhelming. At the moment you may feel fine, there may be little that is causing you stress. But most projects have periods of difficulty and aggravation: it is important to know how you will approach and deal with fears when they arise.

It is worth reflecting on the fears you have as you take on more responsibilities. Do you feel excited about tackling and overcoming them? You may feel nervous and a little trapped by the thought of those responsibilities. When you take a step back, are they big fears with significant consequences, or are they more day-to-day apprehensions with relatively minor ones? What is important is that we are conscious of what we are fearful of, conscious of what the context needs, and that we respond in an appropriate and timely way.

How do you cope with your fear? What are your reflex reactions and how successful are they? It is helpful to have someone with whom you can talk about your fears. This may be someone within the organization who knows the situation well, or may be someone far removed. Either way, you need to trust that they can receive the information in confidence and are able to both support and challenge you. To have someone say, 'Have you thought about how you might handle this fear?' leads you to think constructively. Depending on your personality, you may have gone three, six or twelve months without addressing this fear.

Often we fear things we do not understand. Having a plan in place for the worst that can happen can go a long way to alleviating our fears. Many banks have a recovery office set up to ensure no disruption in service should there be an earthquake, terrorist attack or similar. This step is likely to be too extreme for many businesses, but the principle of careful, contingent planning stands.

It is worth taking time to think about what are the major risks that could arise in your role. What if sales dip, or if a key team-member leaves? What action will you take and what are the long-term consequences for the organization and for you? It is important to have a Plan 'B', otherwise we find ourselves making rushed decisions with little information at crisis points, exactly when decisions matter most.

To what extent do we share our fears with others? As leaders we will have different fears from those under our authority and those in authority over us. You may not want to expose your fears and concerns to the head of the organization, but it may well be prudent to do so.

It is important to be conscious about what fears you are passing on to your staff. Fear is contagious. It can be easy to spread doom and gloom. Equally, staff do not need to be wrapped in cotton wool – they are 'grown ups' too and may well be the leaders of the future. It is prudent to select which fears and issues you share with your staff.

It is sometimes said that fear is a strong motivator, that individuals threatened with redundancy will work harder than those close to promotion. Sports teams battling against relegation often put in incredible performances. We would urge extreme caution about seeing fear as a motivator. In the mid and long term it can only serve to frustrate and exhaust people.

If our fears are realized it may not be disastrous. If the business fails, if your staff leave, even if you are moved on from your role, you can learn, reflect and rebuild. Many successful projects have had crisis points, where all seemed lost and desperate. During such moments there will be feelings of desperation. It is difficult to see beyond the present fear. Yet take heart: it is likely that someone has overcome this type of fear before. You can live through the fear and come out the other side.

---

*When Simon first set up his own business he felt overwhelmed with all the different elements of the project. There seemed to be so many unknowns and variables. So much seemed out of his control. At first this fear was paralysing and he was scared to make decisions for fear of the unknown consequences. He sought advice from a contact who had also set up his own business. They worked through Simon's fears and the risks he was taking on. Although the fear of failure was still present, he now understood its causes and could move forward. He still worried about losing his investment, but at least knew the variables he had to deal with. He was more in control of himself and his own reactions.*

---

## For reflection

- What fears tend to grip you?
- What fears do you need to address as you go forward in this role?
- How best do you handle your fears?

# 14

# Learn how to forgive yourself

We all make mistakes and have moments and decisions that we regret. This is a natural part of life. Stepping into leadership means taking on more opportunities to make mistakes with greater magnitude. Sometimes the worst does happen – businesses fail, projects go sour, supporters fade, employees leave, and we might be made redundant.

But was our time wasted? Was it all for nothing? The answer to these questions does not have to be yes. In almost every circumstance we can rebuild. The future may look different but we can come to a new place by applying what we have learnt from the past.

Whether our mistakes have significant consequences or more mundane effects, there is always the potential either to beat ourselves up or learn and grow from what went wrong. To learn and grow takes conscious effort and is not the easy option. It can be easier to wallow in our mistakes.

Three key steps are: to admit why we got it wrong, to forgive ourselves and to learn and move on. Admitting when we are wrong is about taking responsibility when things are our fault. It is important to think objectively and not just emotionally about the situation, and it can be helpful to ask an impartial advisor what their perspective is. Good questions to ask yourself can be: What exactly happened and why? Was it a known risk? Should it have been a known risk? Sometimes things come out of the blue and cannot easily be predicted. Then it is right to focus on what our response was and could have been. Other questions might be: Whose responsibility was it? Was it 'under your watch'? If fault was with someone under your authority, then you still have to take accountability and a portion of any blame. Do not be tempted to pass on the blame or you may miss the opportunity to learn and might well create enemies.

The second step is to forgive ourselves. We can spend a lifetime wondering 'what might have been' and reliving moments from our past. Unless we learn to forgive ourselves we do not move on. We must first process and let go of the past before we can engage constructively with what is ahead. The greatest sports teams lose matches. Those matches are over and the results can never be changed, but there are always things to learn and more matches to play.

How did you feel when you first found out things were not going well? In the moment all can seem lost, desperate, and panic can set in. With retrospect there is greater clarity. How could you remind yourself of this bigger-picture learning next time you are in a seemingly desperate situation? What is holding you back from moving on? Can you view the situation with 'sober judgement'?

It is hard to be objective when you are in the middle of an unfolding scenario. You need to see things for what they are. You may need to be told by someone else that it is not your fault, or that while you did make a mistake, it is time to move on in your thinking. Wise counsel can be invaluable to help you put reverses into perspective.

The third step is to learn and move on. Often we need to experience depths of failure to understand and learn from them fully. We can explain to a child a hundred times that they need to tie their shoelaces in case they fall. But until the child has experienced falling over they may not understand why it is so important. Until they have grazed their knee on the floor it is purely a boring idea that parents impose.

When an organization is looking for someone with leadership experience, they expect to appoint someone who has experienced tough times and is able to make tough decisions. They want someone who has learnt from experience – someone who knows how to tackle hard problems because they have addressed them before. Being clear about what you have learnt in tough times helps rebuild the confidence you have in yourself and the confidence others have in you.

The same approach can be applied to those under your authority. Developing them is about helping them to take responsibility, to forgive themselves and to learn and move on. Do not be so apprehensive of your staff making mistakes that you do not give them opportunities. Are there opportunities you can give to your less experienced staff that will stretch them, where the risks are not too great yet the potential for learning is high?

---

*After 18 months, Simon's business failed. Although the product and innovations were popular, he simply could not make enough money to sustain himself and the business. There followed a period of self-examination, and Simon was critical of himself for a while. As he conducted the post-mortem, he realized the things he had done well and recognized everything he had learnt from the experience. Once he was able to forgive himself for his mistakes, he emerged stronger and with a fuller, more balanced view of business. He was later able to become a business manager for a large private organization. He was very successful and drew heavily on his experience as an entrepreneur.*

---

## For reflection

- How easy do you find it to forgive yourself?
- What elements of what you have done in your job do you need to leave behind and move on from?
- How best do you move on having forgiven yourself?

# 15

# Be alert to your dreams

What is your dream? What do you aspire to? What is the vision for your team or organization? Maybe it is becoming financially secure, influencing a younger generation, making a difference in a chosen area or providing for your family.

What is the difference between dreams that inspire and motivate and fantasies that lead to a sense of failure, disappointment and disillusionment? Ambition is a good thing. Martin Luther King had a dream about equality for people of different racial groups. Tanni Grey-Thompson had an aspiration to transform the perception of Paralympic sport in the UK and the world. At the time, these dreams would have seemed far off and near impossible, yet they came to pass. The dreams galvanized a generation: action was taken. And the seemingly impossible became possible.

Dreams have the power to bring people together for a common goal. They encourage us to pull in the same direction. They can help to us see through the frustrating parts of our work to something bigger. The dream creates a goal, an end, a focus or a target. Dreams can help us handle those days where we think: What's the point of all this and why did I ever take on this role in the first place? Why? Because you have a dream of something bigger.

It is helpful to have a dream for yourself, but also that your staff have a dream or picture about what might be possible. Why should they persevere on a difficult task? Why should they make that follow-up call to ensure the client is fully satisfied?

Staff may have personal goals. But the more they have a mental picture of what they are striving for, the stronger the likely motivation. But does it feel like a realistic aspiration or a fantasy?

As a girl, Rachel wanted to be an elite runner. She was athletic and felt it was not beyond her reach. Over time it became clear this was a fantasy. Rachel represented her school, but she was not the fastest and her squad was not the strongest in the region. Although she loved to run, she gradually recognized she was never going to become an elite runner.

Fantasies are not rooted in reality and rarely stand up to cross-examination. Do you have a fantasy, which when you think objectively, does not stand up? Maybe it is that 'your team will become best friends' or 'your online brand will get recognized by millions'.

How is your dream going to come about? If that dream will be ten years in the delivering, where do you need to be in three, five and seven years? Are there plans in place to make those steps happen? If you struggle to answer these questions, your dreams possibly need more planning, or possibly they are more like fantasies. These questions can sound boring and frustrating to visionaries, but addressing them helps to avoid future disappointment.

A realization that your goals are unobtainable can be hurtful and knock your confidence if not approached constructively. If you find yourself with unrealistic dreams you might ask yourself: 'Is this still the direction I want to go in? How could this direction be modified to be more realistic?' Perhaps a more realistic goal could be: 'My team is comfortable in each other's presence and open about their struggles' or 'Via various market avenues my brand will get recognized by 10,000 this year and 25,000 next'.

It may be right to drop your dreams entirely and move in a new direction. This may be difficult as you let go of deeply held ideas. We would encourage you to take on new dreams that are ambitious and exciting but rooted in reality. Talking through what these new dreams might be with an objective and supportive friend can be valuable.

What if our dreams are not realized? Is everything lost? Often the answer is no. In pursuit of the dream we are likely to travel much further than otherwise. Maybe you have not won a gold medal, but you still have bronze to be proud of. There is great opportunity to learn from the past, whether the dreams turned into reality or not.

> *As Simon reflected on his time running a business, he realized he had carried a number of unrealistic dreams through the process. He had been fixated on making a quality product, and his perfectionist nature had driven him to focus too much on the details. He had unrealistic expectations on costs and availability of funding. His artistic mentality meant he was not business savvy enough, which had eventually brought down the project. In his future role as a business manager he remained a visionary, but had a clear grasp of short-term realities and necessities. He used his experience to encourage his staff to aspire to big things, while guiding them through the process of achieving them.*

## For reflection

- What dreams of yours are helpful sources of aspiration and energy?
- What dreams are more like unhelpful fantasies?
- How best do you know whether a dream is unhelpful and unrealistic?

# 16

# Be mindful of your foibles and preferences

We all have our own idiosyncrasies. Our own small preferences can make the difference between efficient work and too high blood pressure. For some these preferences cover small things, such as the exact type of coffee or bagel filling. For others a five-minute walk at lunchtime is enough to see them through a stressful day. In this chapter we explore these preferences and foibles, on a day-to-day level and on a longer-term scale. While some of these smaller preferences can seem ridiculous and a touch bizarre, they can be important in freeing us to do the work we want to do. It would be a pity if the absence of a cup of tea meant that poor decisions were made.

Think about a typical day for you. What would you prefer not to do without? How practical are those idiosyncrasies or patterns to your day? If they can be worked into your day, then try to slot them in. If you need half an hour at the beginning of the day by yourself to focus on e-mails, then seek to schedule that in.

It is worth reflecting on when you are at your most creative and when you are at your best tackling tough decisions. Perhaps you can alter the rhythm of your day to accommodate those preferences.

There will be some decisions where you will need to be at your best, particularly surrounding strategy and personnel. How can you ensure you are in the best frame of mind to make these decisions? Perhaps clarifying your thinking is best done out of the office or while walking to get a coffee. Perhaps you are a verbal processor and need the help of a listening ear to organize your thoughts. Whatever your preference, allow yourself to make the key decisions in a way that you are comfortable with.

As a leader you are putting yourself in a position of responsibility for a series of outcomes. Often that comes with the acceptance that lots will happen outside of your control. The question is not how to avoid these offputting situations but how best to respond when they do happen.

Many things can upset your rhythm. These could be external events, staff members, transport problems or an argument at home. How can you re-find your focus and confidence? Perhaps you need to take a few minutes to have some peace. Maybe it is reminding yourself of your achievements so far. Keeping your equilibrium is not about emotional venting at your staff or, worse, at members of your family. Keeping equilibrium is about gaining perspective, being able to take a step back and often learning to laugh at the situation.

We need to be aware of our longer-term preferences and foibles. The same pattern of helpful and unhelpful rhythms is true over a longer period. We may find ourselves coping fine one month, but without regular patterns to revitalize us we may become worn down in months two and three and lose our energy and focus. It is easy to get consumed with the day-to-day and lose clarity about the long-term direction. It is important to remind yourself of the patterns you need to put in place to keep focus, including planning breaks and holidays.

Your staff will all have their own sets of preferences and foibles. Knowing what they are can enable you to put in place weekly rhythms that can keep their energy high and distractions low. Helpful questions can be: If the pattern of work remains the same for the next two years, how would your staff respond? Are they comfortable in their routine or desperate for variety?

If we can take responsibility for our fears and foibles, while sitting lightly to them and learning to laugh at them, we can move forward in confidence. If we strive for perfection and cannot accept anything less, we are likely to be battling our foibles or becoming insecure and discouraged.

We are human beings, warts and all. You will inherit a mixed group of staff. A healthy understanding of your own idiosyncrasies will help you recognize and respond to the idiosyncrasies you see in others. As we understand more deeply the realities of ourselves and our context, we start to react better to the challenges we face.

> *Simon found that the first two hours of the day are his most productive. What he wanted to do was be alone in his office and work on strategic issues facing his department. But the nature of the job meant that his staff often had urgent questions about that day's work early in the morning. This left him frustrated and feeling he did neither type of task well. After discussion with a colleague in a similar leadership role, he talked the issue through with his staff. They were understanding of the conflicting pressures and came to an arrangement where he had one hour to himself each morning barring any particularly urgent queries.*

# For reflection

- How aware are you of your preferences and how can you use them to best effect?
- What foibles do you see in your staff?
- What foibles that you see in yourself do you need to address and move on from?

# PART 5

# Moving up a level

After a period of six months to a year it is good to review how you are progressing in a leadership role. It is always helpful to look back at the progress made, and then to look at potential opportunities going forward. As you review, it can be valuable to think in terms of moving up a ladder, each rung being another step in building credibility. You can afford to be more assertive, while recognizing that it is important to be taking people with you.

This part covers setting the direction, being willing to take responsibility, making decisions well, keeping up communication and knowing how you handle conflict. These five areas are key to becoming established as a leader who is building a reputation for the quality of his or her leadership.

# 17

# Set the direction

Setting the direction is not about picking a long-term aspiration and declaring it to be an inviolate target. Setting the direction is about building a shared understanding of future opportunities and a broad acceptance of the direction of travel.

Sometimes the direction for you and your team is imposed from above or is determined by external events. But you will still have some scope to decide how you move forward in that direction. On other occasions you will have more freedom to set the direction.

In either situation you need to take responsibility as leader in the knowledge of where other people are coming from and having as many interests on board as possible. It is important to create space to stand back and reflect on how you use your discretion to best effect in setting the direction. This might include doing a brainstorm with your boss, or an away day with your team facilitated by a coach or consultant.

It can be very helpful to work through with your team what are the opportunities that are opening up and what the future might look like in two to five years. Ideally you are looking ahead four to five years to create an understanding of where you want to get to. In some cases it can only be realistic to look ahead one to two years.

Developing a vision for the future can be a stimulus for some and a turn-off for others. For some, having a vision is a helpful motivator. For others it is a distraction from getting on with the day-to-day work. Hence the importance of pitching carefully the question of where it is right to make your future contributions and impact, and to do it in a way that recognizes what is going to be helpful to the team.

Even those who are sceptical about the language of vision are likely to engage with discussion about future challenges, opportunities and barriers. Agreeing a set of key principles for the future may be as far as some individuals are prepared to go.

The process of enabling people to imagine what are the future opportunities, if certain short-term issues are solved, can help generate a new freshness in tackling those short-term issues. Enabling people to look beyond the immediate to see that there could be opportunities is the first step to enabling individuals and teams to be 'freed up' enough to think it is worth setting a future direction.

Setting a direction is not about vague theory. It is about defining some practical aspects of what individuals and groups are trying to achieve and then establishing some key milestones along the way. A sense of direction, if it is to be influential, needs to be clear, memorable and not over specific. If it is too detailed, it will be regarded as too precise to be realistic. If it is too vague, it will be regarded as woolly and irrelevant. A sense of direction needs to be visual for those who remember pictures rather than words. It needs to have an emotional dimension for those who remember emotions rather than facts.

A sense of direction can be both about outcomes and how we work together. A team might build a vision of how they are going to work effectively together that covers both how they organize their time and also the type of behaviours they are going to use in relation to each other. The direction they set may involve being more strategic in their discussions and less bogged down in detail. Their declared intent might be to be more willing to challenge each other and not be defensive if concerns are raised.

A clear sense of direction for a team will be about the broad outcomes they want to deliver, the impact they want to have, the way they are going to work together effectively to deliver those outcomes, and how they are going to review their own progress.

Standing back to think about the direction you want to set can be both liberating and create a weight of responsibility. It is liberating to think beyond the immediate to what might be possible, but it also creates a sense of responsibility to use time and energy in a focused way to reach those outcomes.

Once a direction is set it brings clarity of intent, but always needs to be reviewed on a periodic basis. It may feel humiliating to say that the initial direction of travel needs to be altered, but being responsive to the changing context is a critical part of leadership. When the direction is changed, your credibility may be in question, hence the importance of the rationale being a valid and valued response to the changing context.

---

*Jeanette had recently taken over as chief executive of a small charity. She had her own clear ideas but judged that the right first step was to seek the views of the trustees, and to engage with her staff about their perspectives. She was able to build a set of principles for the future direction of the charity that responded to the views she had heard. She worked closely with the chair of the charity to agree a simple, clear statement of intent. There was a shared view about the direction of travel that, over time, helped unify and motivate both the trustees, the staff and wider supporters of the charity.*

---

# For reflection

- How clear is the direction of travel for you?
- How do you want to build a greater shared sense of the direction of travel among staff and supporters?
- What more might you do to ensure that you set a clear, easily understood sense of direction?

# 18

# Be willing to take responsibility

Setting direction may seem tough as you build a way forward with other stakeholders whose support is necessary for success. The corollary of setting direction is the willingness to accept responsibility when you need to drive things through, deal with things that go wrong or handle situations where it feels like there is one reverse after another.

Sometimes you have to stand alone. Your boss is holding you accountable, or you are the only person who can sort out an issue. You are in the firing line and you have to soak the fire, accept responsibility and live with the consequences of that responsibility.

The privilege of leadership comes from the opportunity to play a leading role in setting direction. The responsibility of leadership is to be accountable for your actions to others and to yourself. To survive and flourish as a leader you have to delegate responsibilities for tasks to others but you retain accountability for the effectiveness and efficiency of your organization. If something goes wrong, you will want to review the reasons to find out what happened and put in place corrective action for the future. This is about living your accountability and not denying it or blaming others.

There are times when taking responsibility means driving things through. There is a deadline for the completion of installing a new IT system. The contract is clear and the task has to be completed. Your job is to be focused and do all that is necessary to ensure the task is completed. You will need to be relentless and demanding, overriding people's personal preferences.

Driving things through will be setting expectations that are required to be delivered. As far as possible you are doing this through creating shared expectations. But there are times when you have to rely on the authority of your position or your reputation to insist that certain things are done. If you adopt this approach all the time, it will alienate others. But it will normally be accepted when it is clear that driving something through is necessary. Do not shy away from driving things through when that is clearly needed and you have the underlying goodwill and support from others.

When you believe something needs to happen, you have to put your points simply and clearly, taking necessary time to talk to people individually and in groups. If you are clear and logical in your reasons you will normally gain respect for your perspective, even if others do not agree. If opposition persists, you need to recognize your motives and whether your perspective needs to change. Do not dismiss opposition out of hand. Everyone will have their perspective for a reason, which it is important to seek to understand.

Sometimes you have to stand alone. You have to be accountable to the Parliamentary Select Committee or the audit committee or the charity trustees. You have to be ready to take responsibility and set out why you made the decisions you did and demonstrate that you are willing to live with the consequences of those decisions. Standing alone can be a painful process, but you will feel stronger for having done it on a number of occasions.

Some things will inevitably go wrong under your watch. Someone you appointed will fail to deliver. The financial situation may get much worse either for reasons outside your control or because a decision you took has not worked as well as you had expected. A contract is not delivered and you suspect that part of the reason is because you did not establish the right type of relationship with the key interlocutor at an early enough stage.

When things go wrong, a first reaction can be muttering to yourself that this was not your fault and is not your responsibility, but as it happened on your watch you have responsibility for the way you respond and the next steps you take.

When a decision of yours has proved to be wrong, taking responsibility is not about beating yourself up and cowering in a corner. It is about recognizing the facts of the case, accepting the part you played and then focusing on what now needs to be done. Reverses happen: they are a fact of life. The more we are able to come through situations with our head up high, the better equipped we are for future reverses that will happen, whether we like it or not. If we can genuinely believe that as a consequence we are strengthened and become better equipped to be effective leaders, then we will be able to sit calmly with reverses and believe that the steel in us is becoming strengthened and not weakened.

A key question for any leader is: What is it only I can do? Answering that question gives a starting point for where you need to take personal responsibility about what you contribute as an individual. What it is that only you can do may be about ensuring key relationships are in the right place, or making key decisions on appointments or financial allocations. As a leader, something you uniquely do is set the tone for an organization. Accepting your responsibility to set the tone and recognizing the ripple effect of the tone you set is central to creating a culture where others will accept responsibility and know they need to deliver on their commitments.

Sometimes when you are in the firing line you have to accept that the bullets will pierce your skin. You have to soak up the fire. This might mean acknowledging that you made a mistake. It will mean drawing on all the courage within you to handle the bullets or the fire and keep upright. You will need to draw on your setbacks, but once you have come through the fire, you are hardened by it and better equipped for future reverses.

> *Jeanette made some early decisions about the use of resources that did not work as well as she had expected. A targeted fundraising campaign had not been successful. The trustees began to ask what had gone wrong. She had followed the recommendations of others as she had only been in post for a few weeks, but she recognized that she was accountable and needed to accept responsibility. She was clear with the trustees about why she had made these decisions. Her openness and her willingness to learn reinforced her credibility with both the trustees and her staff. Having demonstrated that she was able to handle something that had gone wrong, Jeanette felt confident that she was in the right role.*

## For reflection

- What do you need to take personal responsibility for driving through?
- What are the things that only you can do?
- How best do you ensure that you take personal responsibility for things that go wrong in a way that enables you to grow in stature and reputation rather than be diminished by what has gone wrong?

# 19

# Make decisions well

Part of leadership is being responsible for making and implementing decisions. At times you may feel daunted by the decisions that need to be taken. What helps is taking one step at a time. You need to have clarity about when a decision is for you to take and when it needs to be made by the Trustees or Board or senior team. Even when the decision is for you to make, how best do you build an understanding with others that you are making the right judgement on their behalves as well as your own?

Some decisions have to be taken quickly in emergencies but most do not have to be made instantly. Time for reflection and discussion is normally highly desirable to enable a considered decision to be reached that you are comfortable with and happy to implement.

Sometimes it can be helpful to imagine you have taken a particular decision and then see what your emotional reactions are and whether you feel comfortable or uneasy about it. You may continue to have some hesitations, but imagining you have taken the decision one way and then the other way, and seeing what your reactions are, can give you good insights. Sometimes it can be helpful to reflect on your learning from making decisions in the past, either at work or in your personal life.

Some decisions are worth making reasonably quickly if they involve no or modest expenditure. A lot of time can be wasted talking about the pros and cons of some decisions where it is more important to get on with it. Other decisions may need significant investment of time and thought, such as those involving people, major expenditure or significant changes of direction. Giving some time for the unconscious mind to be doing the reflecting is never wasted.

It is always worth reflecting on what decisions you are putting off and whether the delay is for good or bad reasons. Sometimes garnering more information and views is essential before a wise decision can be taken. On other occasions we can procrastinate because of uncertainty or a slight fear of the consequences. There will always be a level of uncertainty. Making decisions involves a sense of judgement, even when we have weighed up the evidence and views carefully.

We will not get every decision right. If we get 80 per cent right we are probably doing well. When a decision has clearly been wrong, admitting the mistake and changing direction expeditiously is what is needed. On other occasions we have to live with our mistakes, knowing that we have affected people's lives in a way that we now think was misconceived. Living with our mistakes is never easy, but is part of taking on leadership. Even when we make mistakes that affect people's lives, they are making choices too and the accountability is rarely solely on our shoulders.

Ways of developing your ability to make decisions well might include observing others making decisions, building up your own understanding of where you make decisions well and less well, and getting feedback from others about how the decisions you have taken have been received. Having one or two people who are willing to act as sounding boards when you make decisions will always be useful. But remember that you must take responsibility for your own decisions and not be overly swayed by the strong views of others who do not fully appreciate the context.

Jeanette knew that in the light of the direction agreed for the charity, the mix of staff was wrong. She needed to let a couple of staff go and recruit some others. She knew as chief executive she had to take accountability for making a couple of staff redundant. She thought carefully about this decision and talked with the trustees. She recognized the pain that would be created. She imagined what would be the consequences of the decision for the two people involved. She prepared carefully both practically and emotionally. When she had the conversations, neither person was surprised. One had already made plans for alternative next steps; the other rather grudgingly accepted the inevitable. Jeanette hoped the decision would work out fine for these individuals, but inevitably there was uncertainty for them. She was able to live with her decisions as they were the appropriate consequences of the new direction for the charity. She felt that she had implemented the decision honestly and fairly.

# For reflection

- What significant decisions need to be taken and how are you going to tackle them?
- How best do you draw on the advice of others when you make decisions?
- What practical steps can you take so you are less daunted by decisions that need to be made?

# 20

# Keep up the communication

A key requirement for any leader is to keep communicating. Never believe that when you have said something once it will have been heard. Relentless repetition of the message is essential. People may well not hear or absorb the message the first time. There might be too much noise in their minds for them to receive what you are trying to communicate. Often it is about using the same words again and again so they become part of the litany of the organization. On other occasions it is making the same point in a variety of different ways so that it is impossible to ignore the type of points you are making.

Good communication is about both content and tone. What people absorb from communication is often more about emotions than the content. Clarity and simplicity about the messages is paramount. It might seem tedious to explain a message with three words beginning with capital 'R', but it might mean they are easier to remember and, therefore, have greater impact.

The best communication is often about one simple point expressed in a range of different ways. On other occasions you might have three interconnected messages to get across. Move beyond three and you are likely to lose your audience. An organization that has a change programme based on six principles is unlikely to engender huge commitment as people will not remember six principles. They might remember three key words, but six key principles will get lost, confused and mixed up.

Good communication is about using a range of different means to get your message across. Wherever possible it is based on personal contact – the message delivered face to face is much more likely to have an impact than through a written text. If you have a difficult message to give it is always best to do it face to face and not hide behind an e-mail. An e-mail that is ill-tempered or not thought through is a permanent record, even if you regret it subsequently.

The combination of oral and written communication must be right as it reflects the learning approaches of different individuals. Even in written communication it is the emotions that are engendered that will have the biggest impact. If there is a tone of encouragement, inspiration, hope and joint endeavour, that is much more likely to lead to success than just rational argument. Leaders who think that they will win people over by the power of their logic alone are destined for disappointment.

Effective communication starts from recognizing the needs and perspectives of individuals. Good communication engages with their hopes and needs so that the result is the strengthening of intent and motivation. The key question is what effect the communication is having on the attitudes and behaviours of individuals, not whether it technically looks good.

Each generation is adapting to new forms of communication. As leaders we need to keep up with the rapidity of changes using texting and social networking to best effect. The text message can be such a simple and clear way of communicating. Social networking is for some an effective way of building a shared understanding about where different groups of people are coming from. However, it is only on one dimension and needs to be supplemented by personal contact. Be wary that any contribution via social networks has the potential to reach an unintended audience. A throwaway comment has the potential to go viral and significantly damage your reputation.

A pitfall that awaits many is to assume that the fact that they have sent an e-mail demonstrates they have communicated effectively. If we think that communication is despatching messages, we are likely to be disappointed. Communication is about interaction and engagement, where we are open to our thinking changing. We are communicating well if our thinking is developing because of interaction with others. We are communicating well if we hear others begin to give similar messages to the ones we have been seeking to engage others with.

> *Jeanette needed to raise the profile of the charity. Her first thoughts were to devise some new leaflets and have a mail-out campaign. The chair of the trustees suggested that first she should talk to a cross-section of donors and see what they were interested in and what might encourage them to give to the charity. Jeanette's dialogue with both donors and beneficiaries of the charity encouraged her to develop different ways of capturing the imagination of potential donors. The result was some workshops, lunches with potential partners, presentations about the work of the charity, as well as the production of some focused and attractive literature and the better use of the charity's website. The campaign was a success because of the variety of communication approaches used. When people began to 'tweet' about what the charity was doing, she knew the communication was working.*

## For reflection

- How comfortable are you with a range of different forms of communication, both oral and written?
- How much do you need to build two-way engagement into communication so that it is not all one-way?
- How deliberately do you use different forms of communication with different age groups?

# 21

# Know how you handle conflict

Some of us thrive on conflict while others of us seek to avoid it. Some start from the perspective that unless there is an element of conflict there is not likely to be a creative outcome. Others feel that if there is conflict, the process of trying to agree a way forward has broken down.

There needs to be the opportunity for more than one point of view to be expressed, so that different approaches can be scrutinized. But debate that is overdone and makes people defensive can easily lead to stalemate. Unbridled conflict is usually destructive, but if the boundaries are clear about this type of debate then creative conflict can be useful. Most families know that there are safe areas for discussion and other areas that can lead to conflict. In any organization, the leader will recognize where discussion of some topics will lead to conflict. There is a judgement to be made about whether those areas are never entered or whether they are only entered judiciously, after careful preparation.

Sometimes conflict has to be handled head on. If there are disagreements within a team that are getting in the way and contaminating the organization, the conflict cannot be ignored. As a leader you might want to talk to those involved individually or together. After not initially welcoming your intervention, the most frequent response is a bit of embarrassment that minor differences have managed to degenerate into conflict. Sometimes it is about giving advance notice that if a conflict continues then you will intervene. This forewarning approach can give people the opportunity to sort the issue out and thereby avoid your intervention.

When you feel to be in conflict with someone within your organization, the key steps are to be honest with yourself about the causes of the conflict and assess the extent to which you might have caused it. The ideal is finding a way to talk with those with whom you feel in conflict, to seek the common ground and the basis on which you can move forward together. Often the conflict may be more apparent than real, with both of you wanting to find a constructive way through. It may be that an emotional reaction means that the conflict feels more serious than it really is.

Sometimes conflict cannot be avoided as there may be a fundamental difference that needs to be addressed. At the end of the day, the leader calls the shots. There may be occasions when you have to acquiesce in the views of your boss. On other occasions your staff may have to acquiesce in your views. If there is continuing rumbling, a way has to be found through, either by the issues causing the conflict being openly addressed, or by your limiting the scope and impact of the conflict both on the organization and on you emotionally.

It is worth being conscious of what is your default mechanism when you feel under conflict. Is it to become more aggressive or to become quiet and disappear? Being aware of when your default mechanism clicks in can give you early warning of a problem. It also reminds you to reflect on whether your default approach is the one you want to adopt in this particular situation. As leader you need to be sensitive to the needs of the situation and respond appropriately.

Learning how you handle conflict in a way you can live with is one of the key areas of growth for the emerging leader. Handling conflict can be very emotionally draining. It is crucial to find a way of handling conflict that does not sap your energy in a damaging way.

*Jeanette had difficult dealings with Bruce, one of her trustees. Bruce was very single-minded and blinkered in his thinking. Whenever Jeanette introduced a new idea, she felt that Bruce was bristling and about to contradict her. Initially Jeanette kept her distance from Bruce but accepted that she was avoiding the issue. She wanted to be abrupt with Bruce but knew this was the wrong approach. She had to build a common purpose with him, which she knew would not be straightforward: she suggested that she and Bruce work together on a couple of developments. As they were now facing in the same direction, building a plan, Jeanette began to appreciate Bruce's energy in a new way and Bruce recognized her wisdom more. The outcome was an agreed plan and a much better working relationship between them. Jeanette knew there would always be some potential issues with Bruce, but she had found a formula that worked and that enabled the working relationship to operate effectively. To avoid detrimental conflict with Bruce, she knew that she had to create a situation in which the two of them were working together on issues that were important to both of them. Although they did not see eye to eye on everything, they had come to respect each other's contribution.*

# For reflection

- What enables you to handle conflict well?
- What type of conflicts are you avoiding at the moment and what do you want to do about that?
- How best can you handle an impending, difficult conversation?

# PART 6

# Keeping alert

Keeping alert is about being mindful of what is happening around you and understanding the changing context. It is not about rushing in to solve every immediate problem. Alertness is about seeing what is going on in front of you, alongside you and behind you. It is keeping aware of the emotional dynamics, and what is motivating or derailing people. Alertness does not equate to instancy of reaction. The kingfisher is alert and waits in order to choose the right moment to dive for the fish.

This part looks at different aspects of keeping alert, including being clear about the message you give, being mindful of how you influence, maintaining your momentum while watching when you get stuck, and being conscious of how you motivate others. As the leader, you are being watched carefully by all those around you. They are looking for the signals you give.

## 22

# Be clear about the message you give

You are sending out messages all the time through your words, your demeanour and your actions. You may be giving one message through words but entirely different messages through your demeanour or actions. In the long run we are judged by our actions. But it will be our demeanour that is particularly significant in influencing the behaviours of those around us. If we look optimistic, those around us are likely to feel more optimistic. If we look to be in panic, they are quite likely to go into panic mode too. If we look thoughtful and engaged, the mirroring effect will tend to elicit similar approaches from others. If we enter a room looking calm and in control, we are sending a clear message about the behaviour we think is appropriate.

Words of courage will get us so far but deeds of courage will get us further. It is one thing to utter words about the importance of building partnership with potential critics. It has a lot more impact if you as a leader are seen to have built a new partnership with someone who was a critic and it is clear that you are now acting jointly. That outcome gives a powerful signal that it is both right and doable to build very different working relationships with people with whom you have previously been in competition.

When you give messages as a leader, are you giving 'I' or 'we' messages? When the message is 'we' it can be more powerful because it demonstrates that there is a joint agreement that a particular approach is right. If the 'we' word is used when there is not agreement, your colleagues may well regard you as presumptuous in using the 'we' word, which then can prove to be counterproductive.

Often the 'I' word is absolutely right where you are being clear what particularly matters to you. If you are referring to a mistake that has been made or a wrong direction that was taken, the use of the 'I' word demonstrates that you are taking personal responsibility. If the 'we' word is used, in this situation it implies that you might not feel any responsibility for what happened.

Being unambiguous in the message you send is about clarity, simplicity and one step at a time. Too many messages, and those you are leading may feel confused, overwhelmed or unimpressed. If your message is very one dimensional, you may be regarded as being too single-minded and, therefore, blinkered. Sometimes the message from a leader needs to be expressed at more than one level so that it can be interpreted by different people: for some it needs to be very clear and simple, while others want to understand more of the complexities.

What matters is how people understand your message, not necessarily the precise wording of that message. Getting feedback from trusted others about how your messages are coming over is important. If you are not testing the temperature, you might suddenly find that there is a significant reaction of protest that you had not anticipated. Be aware that while you will have a deep understanding of your message, others hearing it for the first time may interpret your words differently.

Getting feedback about how you are coming over is not principally about whether your message needs to be diluted: it is much more likely to be about how the messages that are important to you are communicated so that they are understood in the way you intend.

Keep watching for ambiguities in what you might be saying or doing. You may think you are being consistent, but others might not see it that way. It is right to vary your style and approach with different groups in order to take cognizance of their perspectives and concerns, but there always needs to be consistency about the core of the message, so that you are seen to be authentic and not pushed around by the whims of different people.

It is important to be clear about your values and priorities as well as your boundaries. These boundaries may relate to the way resources (including time) are used, the way people treat each other and the way decisions are made.

You give a very powerful message when you admit you are wrong. Acknowledging when you have changed your mind allows other people to reflect on whether they have made the right decisions and to be willing themselves to admit vulnerabilities or failures. It is only when failures can be admitted and addressed that an organization can move on constructively. Being open about your own mistakes gives others the freedom to be open about theirs and to move forward constructively.

---

*Anish had recently been appointed to lead the marketing team for a magazine publisher. The department had previously been pulled in a number of different directions and the quality of its work had been variable. Anish was clear that the message he wanted to give to the rest of the organization was that the marketing department was going to focus on what was most important for the agency. He did this by building on the best contributions from his department. The messages he gave to his staff were about how much he valued them and the importance of maintaining high quality and responsiveness. Anish kept talking to key customers so that he understood their perspectives and how his staff were coming over. The feedback loop he created enabled the marketing department to be more adaptable and build a reputation for being more responsive to customers' needs.*

# For reflection

- What are the key elements of the messages you want to communicate to your customers?
- How do you ensure both consistency of message and its appropriateness for different audiences?
- What current messages are you giving that need to be altered?

## 23

# Be mindful how you influence

The parent is seeking to influence their child all the time. Occasionally the influence is expressed through an instruction, 'Please do not do that'. More often the parent is using a range of ways of trying to influence the child in a different direction. The techniques used might be, 'Would you like to?', 'Would it be exciting to?', 'You enjoyed meeting George, would you like to do so again?', 'Shall we go and see if the ducks would like something to eat?' The parent is using the power of suggestion to seek to influence the child. They are seeking to draw on happy memories a child has of a particular activity in order to encourage them to do that activity again.

In a voluntary organization the leader may have limited control but lots of opportunity to influence. The vicar or church minister can exercise control over many aspects of church life. If they do this to excess, members of the congregation are likely to move elsewhere. The vicar or church minister who has a growing congregation is much more likely to be an enabler, someone who can draw out the skills and confidence of people within the congregation. Success as a leader is about influencing members of the congregation to take on leadership roles. It is also about influencing those on the fringe to want to become more involved so they are both contributing and learning.

The most basic way of influencing others is through encouragement. We all like to be flattered, although we can normally distinguish between genuine encouragement and flattery that is just a means to an end. Genuine encouragement is not about bland words of thanks, it is picking out particular contributions that are noteworthy and demonstrating that you have taken a personal interest.

Encouragement can be followed by a phase of discussion about how someone's experience and skills can be used more widely. It is not about leading people to a precise conclusion but about opening opportunities and inviting others to think beyond their normal frames of reference. The 'What might be possible?' question could lead to thoughtful conversations about potential outcomes that had previously been dismissed as unachievable or too hard.

Influencing is not about assuming that one word from you will change the whole situation. Some throwaway lines from you might be quite influential but may not deliver the results you had intended. Every sentence you utter might, in the eyes of some, be treated as an instruction even when you are thinking aloud. Being explicit about whether you are sharing open-ended thoughts or giving precise instructions is important so your hearers do not interpret some blue-sky thinking as a set of new instructions.

Influence often comes when people are hearing similar messages from a range of different people. It is not just what you say that matters. It is what you encourage and enable others to say that can be particularly influential. If your words can stimulate a number of people to make similar points, then the range and weight of opinion will begin to have an impact. It was only when enough people felt strongly about the need to ban smoking in enclosed public spaces that the government of the day felt willing to pass legislation banning smoking in public spaces.

Influencing effectively can be a slow process. Some people take quite a time to change their views and are not going to be rushed. A key decision point is when you feel that you have enough support so that the majority view will prevail. You will not get everyone on board in every case: that is a fact of organizational life.

There are some people you will not be able to influence. That is not your failure: they are choosing either not to listen or to stick to an approach that is different from yours. They are making a choice, which it is right to respect. What matters as a leader is that there are enough people whom you have been able to influence so that there is a strong enough common purpose and intent enabling the organization to move forward.

---

*Anish was conscious that two heads of department were very critical of the marketing department. He knew that he had to build a relationship with these two. He listened to them carefully and allowed them to talk their concerns through with him. Anish acknowledged when their criticisms were valid, but also pointed out where the marketing department had done good work. He built an understanding with these two heads of department about where progress had been made and where further improvement was needed. Anish invited the help of these two individuals to give feedback and to help with quality control. He asked one of them to mentor a member of staff in the marketing department. These steps helped change the whole tenor of the relationship. Anish was able to influence the nature of the relationship between the two directorates and the way staff communicated and developed their contribution to the business.*

---

## For reflection

- How have you been influential in the past?
- Who do you need to influence and how are you going to do that?
- How best do you begin to influence a change of opinion within an organization?

## 24

# Maintain momentum and watch when you get stuck

It is difficult to stand still for long. If you do, your muscles seize up after a while. To keep fit you need to keep moving forward physically. If you are not moving forward in your thinking, you are likely to be moving backwards.

If a car engine has stopped working and you are pushing the car to a garage, it is hard to get it moving, but once you get a momentum it is relatively easy to keep the car moving, provided you are not going up a steep hill. A lot of the effort and ingenuity has to go into getting an initiative started. Keeping the momentum going may then seem more straightforward. What may be needed is gentle steering or sometimes a hard push to ensure the momentum keeps going in the right direction rather than veering off sideways.

Sometimes it feels like three steps forward, two steps back. The reality is you have moved one step forward. Accepting that your impact may feel like three steps forward and two steps back is part of becoming relaxed in the way you can have an impact. You might persuade people that a course of action is right, but a few days later a number of participants are not so sure. Recognizing that further discussion is needed is all part of accepting that some people take time to become fully at home with new approaches.

Once you have got an initiative started, you may want to hand it over to someone else to take the next steps. A good leader is constantly using the skills, enthusiasm and expertise of those around them to take projects forward to the next step. This is not about dumping on them or press-ganging them, it is about identifying and catching their enthusiasms so they willingly take the next steps and feel the ownership of taking the lead.

There is a human desire to keep control and ensure you get full recognition for what you do. However, strengthening the momentum of your team or organization may mean letting go of control on a day-to-day basis. You will still be shaping and enabling, but the momentum will come through the day-to-day energy and efforts of others. Leading well is about deciding when you get directly involved in contrast to when you have an oversight and steer others.

Maintaining your momentum is not about getting cross when people do not think and act at the same speed as you. Sometimes it is about recognizing the speed that people are comfortable moving at, and going along with that speed. Sometimes you have to be tenacious. You may feel strongly and have a good level of support, but others keep focusing on the difficulties. You need to keep listening, but maintaining momentum is about drawing on your inner resolve, focusing people on the tasks in hand and being consistently clear about the rationale for what you are doing.

There are moments when you feel stuck. You hit a brick wall of opposition. You may feel like a rabbit in the headlights and not see a way through a particular problem. You may feel drained and exhausted. For all leaders there are moments of feeling stuck, when everyone else seems to be against them or not understand, and their energy has gone. When you feel stuck, take comfort that you are not alone. Look back and see the progress you have made. Stand aside for a while so you are outside the drama rather than part of it. Observe what different players are doing and saying, and try to be amused by it.

Look ahead to see what might be the routes you can take: there is normally more than one path you can use to climb a mountain. What might be a couple of steps you could take that will give you some satisfaction? Maybe it is just parking an idea for a week or two and then coming back to it with fresh eyes.

Sometimes when we get stuck we do not realize what has happened to us. We feel that what we are striving for is absolutely the right thing, even though it has not caught the imagination of others. When we are stuck on a particular course of action, we need to be listening to others who might be gently trying to steer us to modify our approach so we are a bit more flexible and not so rigid. Presenting an idea in a slightly different way may get a more positive response and lead to the same outcomes.

The secret of maintaining your momentum and watching when you get stuck is about being alert, being able to observe yourself and being willing to be flexible and agile, while keeping clarity in your mind about the sense of direction and the principles that are most important to you.

---

*Anish had agreement to a new marketing campaign that he felt needed to be taken forward quickly. Some of his colleagues began to have reservations. He wanted to express irritation but held himself back. He sat down with his colleagues to understand their concerns, and gradually built an agreed commitment to a way forward. Once there was agreement with his colleagues he could let his staff take forward the work, with periodic steering and stocktake meetings with them. When the project appeared to get stuck because of some external comments, he was able to get the team to accept they had made good progress and that there were more opportunities than problems going forward. Anish helped the team work through a period when the marketing campaign was in danger of losing impetus. Once the campaign was a success, the momentum in the team was such that they wanted to get on to the next projects quickly.*

# For reflection

- What can slow your momentum down and how do you handle it?
- How do you keep up the momentum of others without having to be in control?
- When you feel stuck, how best do you handle the situation?

## 25

# Be conscious of how you motivate others

How well do you understand yourself? Knowing why and how we are motivated is an important piece of self-understanding. There are drivers in us that come from our family and cultural background. Our brain has some well-worn channels that reflect the patterns in the way we think and act. There are rhythms in the way we do things that we cannot ignore.

What motivates us is likely to be a mix of living our values, delivering the outcomes that are most important to us, receiving recognition from others and providing resource for our family. Part of our motivation might be satisfying our intellectual curiosity, fulfilling a long-held ambition or finding new ways of solving problems.

Knowing and understanding our own motivations is crucial, especially when the going is hard and there is a risk that our momentum is dropping. Knowing what will motivate us in difficult circumstances enables us to keep up commitment and energy when otherwise some of the enthusiasm and verve may be sapping away.

As a leader, part of our task is to motivate others. They may be motivated by the same things as us, but that is only likely to be true for some of them. In a university, the academic staff will be motivated by the joy of taking forward their subject area and working with students, but the technical assistants may be motivated more by using their equipment successfully.

The staff working within the university catering department will not be motivated at all by the academic side of the institution. Their motivation will be the pay packet and the opportunity that provides to feed and clothe their children.

It is well worth the time to work through with your staff what is motivating them and how you can help them to fulfil those motivations. As you explore with people their motivations, it is important to understand rather than be dismissive of them. Their motivations may be very different from yours, which is a matter for interest and curiosity and not for dismissing.

If it is clear that what will motivate a junior member of staff is recognition and encouragement, then it is worth the invest-ment of doing this on a regular basis. If someone is going to be motivated by the opportunity to flex their hours at the mar-gins for childcare reasons, are you able to respond to that? If someone is going to be motivated because of some focused time you can give to mentoring them, are you able to do that on a periodic and rationed basis?

The question of what will motivate is relevant both to indi-viduals and teams. What will motivate a team is often about seeing the results of their work, feeling valued, having the opportunity to share ideas, being able to work collaboratively and being able to celebrate successful outcomes as a team. If team members feel they have been able to contribute effectively, so that the team's outcomes are more than the sum of the parts, then there can be a strong sense of achievement. This can give a team the motivation and momentum to take on previously daunting challenges.

How successful you have been in motivating others will be evident in the feedback you get from them. When your clients are telling you positive things about your staff, you can take satisfaction that you are playing a part in motivating them. It is always worth remembering that for some people, all they need in the way of motivation are a few words of gentle encouragement and recognition. Others may need more steering, while for others it will be showing that you understand their issues and problems and can enable them to work these through satisfactorily.

> *Anish knew that he was motivated by seeing figures that demonstrated a successful response to a marketing campaign. Other people in his team were motivated by the quality of their printed products, the novelty of the website, the good partnership with key customers, or the regular pay packet. He sought to understand for each member of his staff what were the key factors that motivated them. Anish let that understanding influence the way he encouraged each member of staff. He was also conscious that they were more motivated if their team meetings began with evidence of the success of what they had been doing, be it a visual illustration or a story about the views of others.*

# For reflection

- How conscious are you about what motivates you effectively?
- What might you do differently with different people in your team to motivate them effectively?
- When your team are together, how best are they motivated?

# PART 7

# Embedding your learning

Every week will bring you new experiences. Sometimes they will be thrilling and enjoyable while on other occasions you will feel downcast. You may think, wrongly, that this type of oscillation is only experienced by new leaders. The contrast between moments of elation and moments of gloom is just as poignant for experienced leaders as for new ones.

Leaders who cease to learn from their experiences are likely to become stale and predicable. Embedding your learning is a lifelong experience. This part looks at: keep learning from your experience, keep developing others, keep listening, reflecting and talking, and be ready to laugh at yourself. Only then can you move on with a light heart to the next 'learning experience'.

# 26

# Keep learning from your experience

Learning from experience is not just about learning from what happens in a work context and applying that learning within the job you are currently doing. We are all continually learning from a whole range of life experiences. As a parent you are learning how to steer youngsters and to organize your time and energy when there are many conflicting priorities. Lessons learnt about influencing skills and management of time from within a family are normally highly applicable in a work context. Lessons learnt from working with volunteers in a community organization, a sports club or a church body often read directly across into motivating a range of different people in a work environment.

When you take on the leadership of a significant area, you want to do everything right. You feel an obligation to those who appointed you to fulfil the belief they had in you, but you will not always get it right. If you are 80 per cent right that is a cause for celebration. Learning from mistakes is part of the leadership journey. Far better to be willing to make decisions and learn from them than find you are recoiling from making necessary decisions.

Keeping on learning from experience is also about observing how others are leading, and observing what works in relation to you and what does not. Who is influencing and motivating you? Who do you take seriously and who are you ignoring or circumventing? The more you can observe other leaders and draw lessons from what is working or not, the more you can be refining your own approach.

In the heat of the moment, when we are under pressure to act, we sometimes do not draw fully on the range of experiences that we have had. It can be helpful to think back to when you might have been in a similar situation before: how did you handle it then and what did you learn about yourself from that experience, and how best do you handle that type of situation in the future? If you are about to have a difficult conversation with someone, taking a few minutes to reflect on how you handled a similar, difficult conversation can both remind you of practical approaches and enable you to calm down your emotions and keep them in check.

A leader taking on responsibility for 30 people for the first time was surprised by how seriously he was taken. Gone were the days when he could joke with other colleagues about what would happen if he made outrageous comments in meetings. The leader was learning that even his throwaway lines were taken seriously and now had deeper significance.

It can often take new leaders a while to accept that they have a new level of authority that needs to be used with care. Their comments or questions will be responded to seriously and they can be surprised by how much influence they have. For some, there is a risk of recoiling from that influence. For a few, the sense of authority might go to their head and mean they become more assertive than is desirable.

In the past, when you gave a talk you might have had a full text, but would like to be able to give a talk without notes. You recognize that learning comes one step at a time, so you experiment with notes rather than a full text. Then at an informal gathering you experiment using a card with ten headings on it. With the confidence that comes from successful experimentation, you use the ten-headings technique with gradually larger groups. Perhaps surprisingly, the technique works.

If you are facing a demanding month looking ahead, it can be helpful to write down what type of approaches you want to use, what you want to observe in yourself, what you want to learn over the next few weeks and what you might experiment with. Then a few weeks later, deliberately looking back and reviewing what has gone well and what has gone less well can help crystallize the learning. Over time we develop different techniques in influencing others, handling meetings or managing our priorities, often one step at a time. We are gradually widening our repertoire of approaches. The key aspect is to be able to embed that learning and say, 'I am making progress.'

> *Esther was nervous about becoming a head of department in a sixth form college. On top of her teaching there was now responsibility for setting the direction for the department and organizing its work and motivating its staff. She knew that there were a couple of disappointed members of staff who had applied for the role she now held. She tried different approaches in talking to them about the work of the department. It took time before it was possible to have constructive conversations: she recognized they had to grieve for a while. Some of her ideas for the department were taken up with alacrity; others got no reaction or were ignored. Gradually she was learning how best to influence and organize her department. The experience was tougher than she had expected, but after three months, when she looked back she recognized that she had come a long way. She was growing into this leadership role and gaining considerable respect and credibility from her colleagues.*

## For reflection

- What have you learnt from your own experiences over the last four months about leading well?
- What are you learning from observing others in leadership roles?
- How can you draw on your experience outside work even more effectively in how you lead others?

# 27

# Keep developing others

As an emerging leader you may feel that you have to keep proving yourself. You have to demonstrate that you can take on bigger and bigger responsibilities and that you are continuing to thrive. You reached your current level because of your own efforts, or so it feels. You have been good at running a project, writing papers, delivering some outcomes or finding new solutions. You have achieved outcomes as an individual that have given you the credentials and reputation to be promoted into your current role.

Often the organization does not need more of the same from you when you have been promoted. Bringing your distinctive, personal contribution will continue to be important, but this might be in very different ways. You may have been promoted because you are a good project manager. Perhaps the key role now is developing your people so they become as effective project managers as you.

You might have been promoted to a senior position in the Probation Service because you were very good at influencing the attitudes and behaviours of young people. Now it is your task to equip and enthuse your staff to do what you used to do well. As a senior accountant, it is now not your job to do the detailed calculations. It is your role to steer others and to build a partnership with the rest of the organization so the work of your staff is influential.

Our first preference is often to appoint people in our own image because we know what they are capable of. We enjoy developing those people who are like us. It is much easier to be communicating with and developing those who think in similar ways. When you take on the leadership of a group there is likely to be diversity in age, experience, aptitudes and motivation. The best teams include a range of individuals who bring different skills and approaches and who are committed to each other's success. Appointing people who are different from you is likely to enhance the team, but may mean that the way you develop and grow them is more of a challenge.

As an emerging leader you may feel daunted to have people working for you who are considerably older than you. Some of them may have a touch of resentment. More often it will be an apprehension about whether their previous experience is going to be valued. Making clear that you value the previous experience of those older than you is always a good starting point. Sometimes it is important to say the obvious and express an interest and appreciation in someone's background, experience and skills. They need to know that you want to use and develop their skills and experience.

You might sometimes think that you learn slowly, but your speed of reaction and learning may be much quicker than some who work for you. Gaining an understanding of the speed at which your people learn and adapt is essential in order to allow you to pace the way you develop them. If your words have a sense of unremitting pushiness, you may quickly leave people behind.

Expressing a sense of urgency may well be important, but it needs to be done in a way that your people think means you are acting responsibly and not panicking. They need to know that you understand the pace at which they and their colleagues can absorb new ideas and approaches, so that they are confident that you will lead them in a focused and wise way.

One of the greatest joys in a leadership role is being able to see people grow. Taking time to mentor and steer can be uplifting and fulfilling. Enabling individuals to take on more responsibility and then seeing them blossom in those roles is one of the most satisfying parts of leading well. The more you can equip people to do the job you currently do so that you become redundant, the better. This can then release you to move on, satisfied that you have developed your people to the best possible effect.

> *Esther appointed two new members of staff, one of whom was straight out of college and the other returning from a period out of teaching. They were both nervous and a bit daunted. Esther spent time with them both, encouraging them and enabling them to think through what they were going to focus on in their lessons. The younger teacher needed Esther's time to be able to talk issues through with her. After a slow start, Esther was delighted to see significant progress in the second half of the first year. The older teacher settled back into her work quickly and just needed occasional conversations to check she was on the right track. Esther used a different approach with each teacher. She wanted to be there so that her advice could be drawn on, but was clear that she needed to keep her distance. At the end of the year it was the way these two teachers had developed that was the strongest cause of satisfaction for Esther.*

## For reflection

- How do you ensure that those appointed bring a mix of different capabilities that contribute well to the overall team?
- Who do you want to enable to develop and grow over the next year?
- What range of approaches are you going to use to develop others?

# 28

# Keep listening, reflecting and talking

You can feel under pressure to take action and get things done. You feel you need to keep your head down and focus on the priorities that are most important to you and to those to whom you are accountable. You might have set yourself some clear targets and feel that it is the delivery of those targets that is of particular importance.

You may feel focused and motivated. Those around you may view you as single-minded or even blinkered or oblivious to what is going on around you. If you keep rushing you might even create a sense of mild panic.

However clear you might be on the sense of direction, it is always important to keep listening, reflecting and talking. It is as we listen that we understand where others are coming from and how our views and actions are being interpreted. Those around you will observe whether you listen to others or whether you listen in order to choose the opportunity to express your views.

The art of listening is about being fully present, recognizing where others are coming from, summarizing back what you have heard and allowing your focus and words to be in a rhythm with the person you are engaged with. Listening is never about blank eyes or a droopy head. It is responding to the mood and tenor of those you are engaged with. The more focused you become, the greater the need to listen with open ears and a warm heart.

Keeping on reflecting is about keeping an open mind so you are continually testing whether your sense of direction and purpose is still right. This is not saying that continuous self-doubt is a good thing, but regularly assessing whether your direction of travel is correct must be the right cross-check.

Good quality reflection can have many different characteristics. Sometimes it is creating a five-minute space when you can reflect, or just turn the brain off. It might involve walking more slowly, or looking at the sky and absorbing the environment around you. As part of a busy meeting, the leader who is confident can suggest taking time out for people to reflect or mull on an issue. We often need to let the unconscious brain process information that it has been receiving. We need to let our rational reactions catch up with our emotional thoughts. Reflection is not a waste of time but a means of enabling us to bring together coherently all the sources of wisdom and insight we are receiving.

Each leader needs to build in a pattern of reflection time that works for them. For some it will be a one-hour stocktake each week. For others it will be a couple of hours a month. For some it might be a day away every six months, alone or talking with colleagues.

Different people will reflect in different ways. Some need a stimulus of written material, others need silence and a blank sheet of paper. For others it is scanning through relevant material on the internet that helps stimulate new approaches and ideas.

Time to reflect and be silent is never wasted, but we need to keep talking too. As a leader we need to be keeping in dialogue with our customers, clients, boss, supporters and staff. Good conversations will sometimes be very open-ended and creative and go where they go. On other occasions it is conversations that focus on a particular issue and different ways of tackling an issue that can be most fruitful. It is through dialogue that we shape others and shape ourselves. It is as we keep articulating what is most important to us that we crystallize our thinking and develop our thoughts.

It can be very informative to look back over a proceeding month or two and assess who you have been talking with and with whom the dialogue has been at its most productive. With those insights it is then a matter of looking forward to see whom it would be good to talk with, both to understand, to influence and be informed and stretched by.

---

*Esther, in her first few weeks, had focused inwardly on her department. She also recognized that she needed to listen and learn about what other people were saying about her department, so she deliberately talked to a range of different people. She took time to reflect on what she had been hearing. There were clear messages that the department needed to be more responsive to both university entrance requirements and to students. Esther knew she had to keep talking with her staff about what she had heard and keep getting them to engage with her about what were the right next steps. For Esther, listening, reflecting and talking had become a virtuous circle in enabling the department to become more responsive and agile.*

---

## For reflection

- Are you listening to a wide enough range of people?
- How might you give yourself more time to reflect in a way that is going to be conducive to thinking ahead?
- How best do you keep up dialogue with a good mix of people?

## 29

# Be ready to laugh at yourself

When something goes wrong, what do you do? Is there a risk that we dig a hole ever deeper and keep justifying our actions or failing to change our perspective? When something goes wrong we can become ever more serious. Our heads can drop and we exhibit emotions that we might regret.

When something goes wrong, the good leader is not shrugging their shoulders and saying, 'That was nothing to do with me'. The good leader is assessing what happened, what the learning is and how things need to change in the future. The good leader is accepting responsibility when they were accountable. They are also accepting the accountability when those to whom they had delegated responsibility have not been able to fulfil all their responsibilities.

Bringing calmness and sober judgement to any situation are characteristics of a leader who has settled into a role well. Calmness is greatly helped if you are comfortable in your values, clear about what matters to you most and supported by family and friends. Keeping a level head and an even temperament, whatever is going on around you, is a precious quality.

Calmness may come through recognizing the inevitability of a particular event or the acceptance that there will always be a diversity of opinion and that it takes time to build agreement about a new direction.

If you feel angry inside, you need to let it out, but in a context and place that you are comfortable with. If you are angry about events or people, it might mean doing physical exercise or taking your brain into a very different place by reading a book on a different topic, or it might mean taking yourself into a very different emotional place by spending time with the family or listening to a humorous story.

Whatever is happening, being able to laugh inside yourself can bring back a sense of perspective and reality. Seeing the ridiculous in any situation can bring us back from the brink of saying something we might regret. Imagining that a difficult meeting is taking place on the top of a mountain in deep snow can bring a wry smile to what might be a sensitive and charged discussion.

Laughing at yourself is particularly important in order to keep learning from what has gone well or less well. If we can laugh about our ineptitudes or crassness, then we can rise above our errors of judgement. The more we can smile at our own quirks the more we can keep a lightness in our attitudes and reflexes.

The more we can train ourselves that when the unexpected occurs, we smile and not grump, the more we will be likely to keep our equilibrium and hold our nerve in difficult situations. Smiling may not be about overt grinning. It might well be an inner feeling of sitting lightly to events. But seeing the amusing side can lead to a twinkle in our eye and a comment that encourages others and sets a constructive tone about not getting bogged down and about taking events in our stride.

---

*By the end of her first year as head of department, Esther was feeling exhausted. There were times when she was feeling agitated that progress had not been as great as she had anticipated, but as she looked back she could see a sequence of changes that were for the best. There had been good progress. With this assurance, there was more calmness as she looked forward. Esther could smile at what had gone wrong. She was able to smile about the situations when she had become too serious and too focused. There were good friends with whom she could share stories about her tendency to get little things out of proportion. She looked to the second year as head of department with both anticipation and a smile on her face.*

# For reflection

- When are you in danger of taking yourself too seriously?
- What in your current leadership role makes you smile?
- How can you create a situation going forward when you smile to yourself more often?

# PART 8

# Taking next steps

This final part invites you to stand back and reflect, and then to look ahead in confidence and expectation. Since you began to take on significant responsibilities as an emerging leader, you are likely to have travelled a long way in a short time. It is now right to take stock and see the journey you have travelled and the pathway ahead.

This part looks in turn at being confident in your developing strengths, developing a clear understanding of your way forward, sitting lightly to uncertainty and building your legacy. As we look forward there is inevitably a mixture of fixed points and uncertainties. Holding firm to what is important to you and sitting lightly to the rest is part of preparing effectively for the future.

## 30

# Be confident in your developing strengths

It is only when you look back that you see the journey you have travelled. We are shaped by the range of experiences we have been through. Looking back we can be surprised by our own progress. We perhaps never thought that we could chair big meetings successfully, lead major presentations or bring difficult negotiations to conclusion.

Moving into a situation where we have to take responsibility means we can grow much more quickly than we had expected. Celebrating the development in what we feel comfortable doing as a leader is important so that we reinforce the sense of personal growth and confidence. Allowing yourself to be surprised is important as it opens up the acceptance that you might be surprised again by your future ability to cope in situations where you are apprehensive.

You may be developing strengths in parallel areas of your life. Taking on leadership roles in a community, sports or faith-based organization can help develop leadership skills that are readily transferred into your workplace. Developing the capacity to lead volunteers can often develop subtle ways of building the motivation of partially interested people who work under your oversight. This is an invaluable skill in any workplace. Leading in other spheres gives you the opportunity to experiment with different approaches and then apply some successful ones in your work context.

Perhaps the most transferable skills come from family life, whether it is encouraging younger children, dealing with rebellious teenagers or handling parents who have become increasingly rigid in their attitudes and behaviours.

Performance reviews are an invaluable way of taking stock, with positive feedback always being encouraging. It is crucial to listen to what people say and do not say. The affirmation of what you are good at gives you a firm basis to continue to build on positive attributes. Explicit comments about areas for development should be a matter for deliberate and constructive thought rather than hurt pride. But what did you not receive feedback on? Had you anticipated positive comments for an activity that you thought had gone well? So why no comment? Were you expecting developmental comments in an area where you thought you had not done so well? Perhaps the absence of comment meant that you contributed in this area to a higher level than you had assumed.

Our own self-assessment may be accurate up to a point. But often we underrate our contribution and fail to appreciate the impact we are having. Often by virtue of the type of tone we set we are having a much bigger impact than we anticipate. On other occasions we can be blinded to, or deliberately blank out, an approach that did not work well. We have to ensure we are honest with ourselves as we draw on the perspective of trusted others.

The good leader always brings modesty and an awareness of the contribution of others. A proper sense of humility is essential for any leader so that power does not go to their head and they are willing to keep learning whatever happens. But excessive modesty is not helpful to the individual leader or the organization they are leading in. You have been appointed to a role because people believe you have the credentials and capabilities to do that role well. Therefore there is an obligation to embrace the leadership responsibility fully and not to protest that it is too difficult.

It is right to bring an accurate appreciation of the strengths and capabilities we bring to our leadership tasks. This is not about flaunting our strengths but about using them well. It is not about saying, 'I am the best', but it is about using your capabilities to ensure the best possible outcomes are delivered.

If we see our strengths as gifts that are there to be used, this perspective can help us use them overtly and responsibly. The gift that is hidden away gathering dust is no good to anybody. The gift that is used to bring pleasure to others and to develop the capabilities of others is precious. The more we can see our strengths as gifts, the more willing we will be to use them in an open way that is modest in approach. It is important to stop excessive modesty getting in the way of deploying the gifts of leadership we have been given.

*Isobel had recently been appointed to a management role within the health service. She was initially daunted by the idea of having to work with very bright and sometimes self-opinionated clinicians, but she knew that she had particular gifts in planning ahead and delivering practical improvements. After her initial few months she received good feedback from the clinicians, who were positive about the skills she brought. When she took stock she was pleasantly surprised by the progress she had made and her ability to persuade clinicians to change their minds. There were still areas for development and she was continually refining the way she influenced the clinicians. She recognized that she needed to celebrate the strengths she had and progress she had made.*

# For reflection

- What has surprised you about your progress as a leader?
- Are you sometimes too modest for your own good?
- What particular strengths do you see as gifts that you would like to deploy more fully?

# 31

# Develop a clear understanding of your way forward

You are busy dealing with day to day pressures. It is hard enough to look two months ahead. Looking five years ahead seems a luxury you do not have time for. But in any stage of life, looking five years ahead can help give a perspective that enables you to do the day job better. Looking five years ahead is both about your current leadership role and your own personal development.

What are the aspirations for your part of the organization? Is your part of it destined to become more significant or less? Is there a growing need for the type of service and contribution that your organization is making? What types of demands are likely to come your way over the next few years? How can your organization best prepare to meet those demands and expectations?

Perhaps it is not possible to answer these questions, but if reflecting five years ahead can give some insights that enable the priorities in your current role to be clearer, then it has been worth doing the exercise. If you think that your part of the organization is going to become less needed, perhaps part of your task is to develop wider skills in your people so that they can move on to other roles.

It is worth looking ahead five years at the skills and competences that future leaders are going to need. If you think the organization is going to become more international or more virtual, how can you develop your skills and understanding so that you can be a key player in however the organization changes and evolves?

If in due course you would like to be a senior leader, imagine yourself in that role and try to experience the type of joys and frustrations that you would then be living. Imagining what it is like to sit in the role of a senior leader can help you crystallize what is the type of experience and learning you need to develop in order to be able to do that senior role well. Perhaps imagining yourself in the role might lead you to think that you need more finance experience or more experience working with a different type of organization. The clues about your own personal development that come from imagining yourself in a senior role can be valuable in steering how you focus your personal development efforts.

It is always worth reflecting on what might be your next role after your current role, which may mean thinking through a number of different options. For each of them it is worth considering how your current role and experience is preparing you for the type of job you might like to do next. This is both about developing confidence in taking on responsibility, and preparing a set of stories about what you have delivered. When you apply for your next job, what will be particularly important are the stories you are able to tell that catch the imagination of the interviewers and demonstrate that you have both the expertise and the confidence to do your next job well.

Building a clearer understanding of the way forward is not just about your personal preferences. Crucial is the perspective of your spouse or partner and the needs and demands of members of your family. What matters most to those closest to you might be that you are at home a lot and able to spend a significant amount of time with your children. In other families what is important is that one of the parents brings in a significant stream of income, even if this means he or she is are not available to spend as much time with the children. Keeping an ongoing dialogue about what are the preferences of significant others in your life is important. There may be a risk of outdated assumptions that need reassessing.

Whatever your hopes and aspirations might be, you rarely get there in one leap. Progress comes one step at a time. Sometimes the terrain is steep and on other occasions it is shallow. If we rush progress too much we exhaust ourselves, but moving purposefully forward, taking opportunities as they arise, is likely to lead to reasonable outcomes.

Inevitably, there will some blind alleys. We chart a particular course and realize it is not going anywhere and have to change direction. But even those blind alleys can give us a different perspective about what is possible and what is unrealistic. When you reach the end of a blind alley, progress is about turning around and retracing your steps without your emotions being clouded by too much angst.

---

*Isobel was clear that some of the systems in the hospital were too rigid. She wanted to play her part in building a more agile and flexible organization in which clinicians were more willing to work positively with administrators. She spent time developing her understanding of changes in medical practice so that she could work constructively over the long term with the clinicians and always have their respect. Isobel and her husband Paul talked through on a regular basis their different career aspirations. They were willing to plan for the future in a flexible way. Both of them ensured they kept developing their understanding about the future shape of jobs in their areas of expertise. It was one step at a time as they kept up their professional development.*

# For reflection

- Is it useful to look five years ahead in your organization to see if that influences your priorities as a leader?
- How does looking five years ahead influence your own personal development priorities?
- Would it be worth having a reflective conversation with close members of your family about what is going to matter most to them and you over the next few years?

# 32

# Sit lightly to uncertainty

However much we plan, the unexpected will happen. We will not be able to predict fully the course of events over the next few years, or even the next few weeks, but it must be right to do some planning ahead. There needs to be clarity of direction and clarity about how both human and financial resources are to be used. But few plans run smoothly. Key people will inevitably move on. The views of customers and clients may change for seemingly irrational reasons. A new boss may be appointed whose approach is entirely different. You had originally felt appreciated, but now you are not so sure.

Even when things are going well, it is worth having both a Plan 'A' and a Plan 'B', and to reflect on how you would react if neither of these plans came to fruition. If we can see uncertainty as inevitable, then we will be less likely to be thrown by the unexpected. The fact that life is uncertain keeps us on our toes and stops us becoming too predictable. If we have to keep alert, to watch out for the unexpected and for surprises, then we are more likely to be able to adapt well to them. The more we can see the unexpected as surprise gift rather than unwanted explosion, we are likely to respond in a constructive way.

There is nothing certain about our health: medical issues are bound to arise from time to time. It is how we respond to health issues that matters. Sometimes we need to stop and slow down for the good of our physical and mental health. Listening to and not ignoring signals about our physical and mental wellbeing is important.

Uncertainty is an opportunity. When there is uncertainty it throws up the need for different ways of thinking and a willingness to bring in fresh ideas that have worked well elsewhere. When uncertainty arises it is often worth asking the question: What are the opportunities that might now arise because of these uncertainties? Those who have fixed views may become less sure of themselves at a time of uncertainty. They may be more open to listening to the views of others, which can enable you to be more influential with them.

We can see uncertainty as a chance for others to shine. If a project is facing problems, there is an opportunity for participants to test out different approaches. Encouraging those around us to use their initiative and ideas to address unexpected problems can lead to a release of new energy and hope.

It is important to trust your own judgement at times of uncertainty, drawing on all your past experience. Sometimes we can fear uncertainty. But if we can look back and see how we have handled uncertainty well in the past and used it as an opportunity to move forward, then we can believe that it will bring out the best in us.

Part of the realism of life is accepting that you will not win every battle. The direction of travel may be clear but it will not always be smooth going. There will be setbacks and disappointments. Living with those setbacks and disappointments is all part of sitting lightly to the unpredictable and the uncertain.

Setting out purposefully to make a difference and deliver what is important to you is serious business. But if we are too serious we can get bogged down, frustrated, annoyed and angry. We need to be able to be both active in the heat of the moment, and able to be above the action and sit lightly to unpredictability and uncertainty. When something goes wrong we need to ensure that we are not too emotionally wound up about what has happened. The right response is to assess what has happened and learn from it, while sitting above it and not allowing one disappointment to be contagious across the whole of life.

*Isobel had to live with the unpredictable behaviour of some of the clinicians. One minute the finances were clear, while the next they seemed uncertain. There were not as many fixed points going forward as she would have liked. But she recognized that there were potential advantages as a result of the uncertainties. The clinicians began to talk to her about how best to handle the financial situation when there were more demands and fewer resources. They began to trust her judgement and recognized that she had an expertise they did not possess.*

*Isobel accepted that she would not win every argument. Sometimes she would have to concede to the clinicians in order to keep up their goodwill and support. She saw uncertainty as a chance to give opportunities for others in her team. After some initial aggravation, she persuaded herself that she needed to sit more lightly to unpredictability and uncertainty. It was a breakthrough when she accepted that not everything was under her control!*

## For reflection

- Can you see uncertainties that might lead to helpful opportunities?
- How might current uncertainties bring out the best in you?
- How might uncertainties provide an opportunity for others to shine?

# 33

# Building your legacy

You may see yourself as having big responsibilities resting on your shoulders. You have a job to do with a set of objectives that may be well defined or a bit vague. You feel responsible for making things happen and are aware that you are being watched and judged.

Your responsibility is not just for the tasks you have been given or have set yourself. There is a wider responsibility to engage and inspire those you work with. As leaders we have a duty of care to ensure that those who work for us feel encouraged and supported, and have the resources available that are necessary for them to do their jobs well. We have a duty to ensure that the expectations upon them are reasonable and that their contribution is acknowledged and rewarded appropriately within the bounds of realism. But our leadership responsibility is much more than a duty of care. It is our task to inspire and enable those around us to step up successfully and be more influential than they had ever thought possible.

Our legacy is not what we do, it is through the actions of our followers. We can influence a whole cadre of individuals through the way we mentor, motivate, steer and encourage. We can create a cascade effect that can mean that our influence resonates through a wide range of different people and contexts. If we can enable someone to become a better project manager, a more rounded accountant, an influential negotiator or a more effective speaker, then we will have created an effect that can be cascaded through the actions and influence of our mentees.

Effective engagement includes creating opportunities for a wide range of different people through the work we do. It might be through raising their expectations and aspirations. It might be through stimulating people to think of new ways of doing things and challenging individuals and groups to leave behind rigid and outdated attitudes.

You will not be able to engage and inspire others successfully unless you yourself are continually looking for new sources of engagement. Who you are going to learn from is a question it is important to keep answering. What different situations are you going to put yourself in so that you will gain new understanding and perspectives?

Your sources of inspiration might come from books, articles, speeches, broadcast material, conversations and your own reflections. Allow yourself to be the recipient of a wide range of inputs. Allow yourself to talk to new people and discuss different ideas.

Keep remembering who has inspired you in the past and who might inspire you in the future. Keep engaging with a cross-section of people you meet, from the non-executive director to the receptionist. Each will bring their own insights and wisdom. All of them can be sources of inspiration as you keep up your momentum about the type of leadership contribution that you want to bring.

Being authentic to yourself as a leader is not about looking at yourself in isolation. Being authentic is about engaging effectively with all the people around you and then knowing how to inspire and motivate them. The emerging leader will rarely have acted alone. They will have built a group of supporters who both work with them closely and support from a distance. The emerging leader will be gradually building followers who will be willing to support them over the years to come.

Success does not come through putting on a particular mask when you talk to particular groups of people. Success comes through your bringing qualities of consistency, compassion, clarity and commitment. The leader who inspires is both careful and courageous. Inspiration is about both inspiring yourself and those you work with. It is about the belief that improvement is possible and that you can make progress, even if it is one step at a time.

Your legacy may seem finite. But if you inspire others who then cascade that inspiration, your influence can be infinite.

---

*Isobel inherited a mixed set of working relationships. She wanted to create a legacy whereby the professional and administrative staff worked well together. She ensured that the respective contribution of all the different groups was understood and appreciated. She created opportunities for people to work together and advance their careers. She spent a lot of time investing in people so that their confidence grew. Isobel was an inspirational presence for junior staff in a variety of different professional groups. She was willing to speak directly when restrictive practices needed to change, but she was also hugely supportive when there were opportunities to improve the quality of services within their tight resource. Isobel was going to be long remembered for her commitment and the generosity of time she gave to engaging with and inspiring her staff and colleagues.*

---

## For reflection

- Who do you think you might have inspired recently?
- What is the legacy you want to leave behind in this role?
- How might you inspire your staff over the next few weeks?

# Books by Peter Shaw

*100 Great Personal Impact Ideas*, London: Marshall Cavendish, 2013.

*Business Coaching: Achieving practical results through effective engagement*, Chichester: Capstone, 2007 (co-authored with Robin Linnecar).

*Conversation Matters: How to engage effectively with one another*, London: Continuum, 2005.

*Deciding Well: A Christian perspective on making decisions as a leader*, Vancouver: Regent College Publishing, 2009.

*Defining Moments: Navigating through business and organisational life*, Basingstoke: Palgrave/Macmillan, 2010.

*Effective Christian Leaders in the Global Workplace*, Colorado Springs: Authentic/Paternoster, 2010.

*Finding Your Future: The second time around*, London: Darton, Longman & Todd, 2006.

*Getting the Balance Right: Leading and managing well*, London: Marshall Cavendish, 2013.

*Leading in Demanding Times*, Cambridge: Grove, 2013 (co-authored with Graham Shaw).

*Making Difficult Decisions: How to be decisive and get the business done*, Chichester: Capstone, 2008.

*Mirroring Jesus as Leader*, Cambridge: Grove, 2004.

*Raise Your Game: How to succeed at work*, Chichester: Capstone, 2009.

*The Emerging Leader: Stepping up in Leadership*, Norwich: Canterbury Press, 2013 (co-authored with Colin Shaw).

*The Four Vs of Leadership: Vision, values, value-added, and vitality*, Chichester: Capstone, 2006.

*The Reflective Leader: Standing still to move forward*, Norwich: Canterbury Press, 2011 (co-authored with Alan Smith).

*Thriving in Your Work: How to be motivated and do well in challenging times*, London: Marshall Cavendish, 2011.


**Forthcoming books**

*Celebrating Your Senses*, London: SPCK, 2013.

*Effective Leadership Teams: A Christian perspective*, London: Darton, Longman & Todd, 2014 (co-authored with Judy Hirst).

*Sustaining Leadership*, Norwich: Canterbury Press, 2014.